Sunset

Patio Roofs
& Gazebos

By the Editors of Sunset Books and Sunset Magazine

**Decoratively cut rafter ends add style to classic patio overhead
(see page 41). Landscape architect: Rogers Gardens.**

Sunset Books ■ Menlo Park, California

Stunning setting contributes to allure of billowy-roofed gazebo. (For plans, see page 64.) Architect: Mark Hajjar.

Garden Shelters

Whether it's a covered entryway that welcomes guests to your home, a good-looking roof over a patio, or a charming backyard gazebo, few landscaping elements can do more to enhance your garden than a well-designed outdoor structure.

This book begins with a short course on planning and designing your own structure. In the project section, you'll find full-color photos and plans for a variety of overheads and gazebos. The last chapter sets out the construction techniques you'll need to know, from laying out the footings to finishing the wood.

It's important to remember that each project shown in this book was designed for a particular site and setting. Since your situation will differ, you'll probably have to adapt the project to accommodate your site, the soil conditions on your property, and any other considerations that could affect design or construction.

We extend special thanks to JoAnn Masaoka for styling many of the photographs, Marianne Lipanovich for location scouting, and Kathy Oetinger for cutting the color screens for the illustrations.

Research & Text
Don Vandervort

Book Editor
Fran Feldman

Design
Joe di Chiarro

Illustrations
Mark Pechenik
Bill Oetinger
Rik Olson

Photographers: Donald R. Belt, 61 (bottom); Dennis Bettencourt, 50; Peter Christiansen, 12, 51, 54; Stephen Cridland, 15; Fry + Stone Associates, 16 (right), 17 (right); Daniel Gregory, 16 (left); Stephen Marley, 5 (right), 52, 58; Jack McDowell, 5 (left), 21, 47, 70; Don Normark, 13, 45; Norman A. Plate, 4, 10, 24, 26, 31, 36, 55; David Stubbs, 66, 95; Michael Thompson, 14; Don Vandervort, 6, 11, 17 (left); Peter O. Whiteley, 38; Tom Wyatt, 1, 2, 18, 22, 25, 28, 32, 35, 40, 41, 43, 49, 53, 56, 62, 63, 65, 68, 82.

Cover: Romantic Victorian-style gazebo offers tranquil garden retreat. (For building plans, see page 57.) Design: Gazebo Nostalgia. Photography by Tom Wyatt.

VP, Editorial Director, Sunset Books:
Bob Doyle

16 17 18 19 20 QPD/QPD 9 8 7 6 5 4 3 2 1

CONTENTS

PLANNING & DESIGN

Like a beckoning friend, a patio roof or gazebo invites you to step outside, away from household noise and bustle. It can be a place for quiet conversations, for after-work relaxation, for reading, or for socializing with friends.

The key is to design a structure that meets the needs of your family effectively and efficiently. To do so, you'll have to analyze various sites around your house, understand your garden's microclimate, and be familiar with legal restrictions in your area.

Then you'll want to put your ideas on paper, either solo or with the help of a professional. For this, you'll do well to study up on your choices of roofing and structural materials—lumber, outdoor fabrics, plastics and glass, solid roofing products, and so forth.

Whether you want to design and build the structure yourself or you plan to hire a professional, this chapter will help you understand the entire planning and design process.

Patio roof draws guests outdoors, expanding home's living space. This overhead creates a feeling of enclosure, despite its minimal structure. Landscape architect: Robert Chittock.

Today's patio roofs, gazebos, and other overheads not only make the outdoors more inviting but also serve as major architectural and landscaping elements. Increasingly popular, outdoor shelters help make gardens, patios, and decks active, integral parts of a home. And while they enhance the enjoyment of outdoor areas, they add visual interest and often increase a home's value.

Overhead structures can have many benefits:

■ *Controlling the sun.* Situated on an exposed patio or deck, an overhead can diffuse the sun, converting a sun-baked surface into a cool, inviting oasis. By casting shade across the house, it may also reduce the sun's glare and even lower air-conditioning bills during the warm summer months.

■ *Shedding rain.* In a wet climate, a solid roof shelters a deck or patio from rain, extending the period during which the outdoor area can be used. In addition, a well-designed solid patio roof can offer cover over doorways or help direct rainwater away from the house. As a bonus, outdoor furniture and equipment can be stored beneath it, safe from harsh winter weather.

■ *Extending livable space.* Patios, poolside pavilions, and garden entertainment structures can draw guests into the yard, taking the strain off your home's kitchen, dining, and living areas. When outdoor entertainment centers are equipped with barbecues, work surfaces, and seating areas, they make entertaining a delight.

■ *Adding visual interest.* A well-designed patio roof or deck overhead can dramatically improve your home's appearance, giving a nondescript roofline a new dimension. At poolside or in the garden, a pavilion or gazebo introduces a dynamic landscape element, a focal point for the balance of your landscaping. A series of overheads can integrate several landscape features, such as a deck, a pool, and an entertainment area.

■ *Increasing a home's value.* A new patio roof or gazebo, if well designed and built with care, will enhance your home's livability and appearance, thereby adding to its resale value.

■ *Enhancing privacy.* If your home is located in an area where houses are built close together, an overhead or other garden structure provides a measure of privacy and a feeling of enclosure. Regardless of the size of your yard, the structure can connect you with the outdoors—with the calm and beauty that nature offers.

THE KEY: CAREFUL PLANNING

When you embark on a home-improvement project, the natural tendency is to want to jump right in and start building. Resist the temptation! With any building or construction project, planning is the most important step. Without planning,

Traditional and charming, this shingle-roofed gazebo makes a handsome focal point on hillside deck and an ideal lookout over lake below.

Sun control is a primary task of many patio roofs. Trellis units on this overhead can be adjusted or removed, depending on amount of sun desired. Design: Tom Silvers.

it's too easy to make mistakes that are costly and frustrating at best, disastrous at worst.

Planning is all the more critical when you're building a structure that will be a major addition to your house or landscape, or one that needs to filter sunlight or shed rain. In addition to developing a design that fulfills your needs and blends with your home, you must consider site, climate, legal restrictions, cost, and myriad other factors.

If you can successfully transplant one of the patio roofs, overheads, gazebos, or garden shelters from this book to your home, great! But it's likely that the soil conditions on your property, the site you've chosen, or even local building code requirements are quite different from those for which a particular project was designed.

Consider, then, how you might modify a project to work for you. Unless you're well trained in design and construction techniques, it's usually best to consult a professional for expert advice on building specifications. For information on working with professionals, see page 9.

Evaluating Your Needs

Before you can begin thinking about the design and construction of your new outdoor structure, it's important to determine the purpose you want that structure to serve.

Together with the other members of your family, try to answer questions like these: Do you need covered areas outdoors where kids can play? Should these areas be within view or connected to the house? Does sun or rain create problems for patios, decks, or interior rooms? Do you enjoy entertaining outdoors, and, if so, do you need better facilities for it?

Address the big picture first, discussing how you might develop an overall landscape plan. Consider how your family's needs are likely to change over time and think about any outdoor additions you may want to make in the future. Be realistic about your resources, but don't hesitate to think big. Even if you can only afford to attack one problem now,

a comprehensive plan can help you achieve a complete, harmonious result later on.

As your rough ideas take shape, hone them into specifics, gathering as much information as you can. Study the projects in this book to see how they might meet your needs. Flip through home-improvement magazines and other idea books, and observe how neighbors have met similar landscaping challenges. For ideas on patios, walkways, and other landscaping elements, see the following *Sunset* books: *Garden & Patio Building Book, Decks,* and *Patios & Decks.*

General Design Considerations

Good design is crucial to the success of any outdoor project. Not only should the structure not block desired light or views, but it also must harmonize with the architectural style of your home. The structure needs to set the right mood without looking as if it were tacked on.

A good design should take its cue from your home's architectural style. If your house is a Victorian, for example, classic crisscrossed lattice would be an

appropriate material for an overhead. If your home has a feeling of openness, so should a trellis that's part of its outdoor space.

Though it's not essential that an overhead near the house be built from the same materials as the house, the new structure should blend harmoniously with it, rather than create a jarring contrast. Colors need to be complementary, too. It may also be important how an outdoor structure flows from the interior space.

Consider sight lines. When you're standing inside looking out, beams that are too low will pull your viewable horizon down. It's important to plan the overhead's height so it doesn't block a nice view. Generally, it's best never to place the lowest beam less than 6 feet 8 inches from the finished floor surface.

Choosing a Site

For many overhead projects, the site is predetermined. You may have only one deck or patio—with no intention of building another—and that is where you need shelter from the elements. The spa overhead will go over the spa, the pool entertainment area next to the pool.

Vine-covered attached patio roof echoes design of house in both style and color. Landscape design: G. Grisamore Design, Inc.

Plotting the Sun's Path

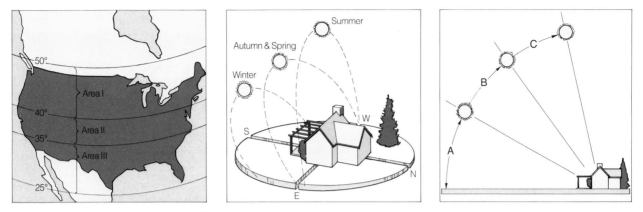

Shade is cast at various angles, depending on time of year and where you live. Find your location on map above and refer to chart below, at right, for sun angles on your property.

If, on the other hand, your site is more flexible or you're developing a comprehensive landscaping plan, you'll want to review a few basic site considerations. (For information on legal restrictions, see page 8.)

Relationship to the house. As you consider different locations for your overhead or gazebo, evaluate each site in terms of its accessibility from the house, any established traffic patterns from house to yard, views you want to preserve from inside the house, and overall convenience. Of course, your primary concern should be to locate your structure where it best meets your needs. Otherwise, it may not be used.

Relationship to the yard. Every piece of property is different. Study your yard—its contours, views, the location of trees, and any other relevant elements—and try to maximize its assets. At the same time, don't ignore any problems, such as drop-offs, areas that drain poorly or have unstable soil, and exposures to blazing sun or strong winds.

Because choosing the right site is so important, you may want to consult a soils engineer, a landscape contractor, or a design professional for help.

Knowing Your Microclimate

In order to get the most use from any outdoor area, you must understand its microclimate. Sun, wind, and rain affect different parts of your property in different ways. Moreover, buildings, trees, and other obstructions on or near your property can all have an impact on your garden's microclimate.

If you've lived in your community for a number of years, you probably have a fair idea of the general weather conditions—average seasonal temperatures, rainfall and snowfall patterns, prevailing wind directions, and the number of sunny days. If you don't, ask neighbors who are longtime residents.

What you may not know is how much sunlight falls on your deck in July or from what angle the summer sun streams into your bedroom. If you're planning to build an overhead to control the sun, you'll need this kind of information.

The sun's path. Theoretically, a patio that faces north is cool because the sun

rarely shines on it. A south-facing patio is usually warm because, from sunrise to sunset, the sun never leaves it. Patios on the east side stay cool, receiving only morning sun, while west-facing areas can be uncomfortably hot because they absorb the full force of the sun's mid-afternoon rays.

But there are exceptions to these general rules. In hot areas of the country, north-facing patios could hardly be considered cold in the summer. And a west-facing deck in San Francisco is rarely hot because stiff ocean breezes and chilly fogs are common during the summer months.

The sun crosses the sky in an arc that changes slightly every day, becoming lower in winter and higher in summer (see illustration above, center). In the dead of winter, it briefly tracks across the sky at a low angle, throwing long shadows; on long summer days, it moves overhead at a very high angle. The farther

SEASONAL SUN ANGLES

Season	Sun's Position/Hours of Daylight (see map above)		
	Area I	**Area II**	**Area III**
A Noon, 12/21	21°/8 hrs.	29°/9 hrs.	37°/10 hrs.
B Noon, 3/21 & 9/21	45°/12 hrs.	53°/12 hrs.	60°/12 hrs.
C Noon, 6/21	69°/16 hrs.	76°/15 hrs.	83°/14 hrs.

north you live from the equator, the more dramatic the difference.

Dealing with rain and snow. When planning a shelter, consider the effects of rain and snow. If you live in an area that experiences heavy snowfall, your overhead structure must be able to handle the snow's added weight. You'll also have to consider where the runoff from the roof will go. For help, consult a design professional.

Legal Restrictions

Before you get too far into the planning process, contact your local building department to learn about the regulations that apply to outdoor structures in your area.

In most localities, a house-attached patio roof must meet building code requirements, and a building permit must be obtained. Freestanding, detached structures may or may not be regulated. In addition, zoning laws normally govern whether or not such a structure can be built on your land and restrict where it can be located.

Building codes set minimum safety standards for materials and construction techniques, such as the depth of footings and foundations; the size and type of posts, beams, and other structural members; and steel reinforcing in foundations.

Building permits are often required, depending on the project's size, whether or not it's a house-attached roof, and its intended use. Projects entailing electrical wiring or plumbing may require separate permits for each task. Check with your local building departme and be sure to get any required perm

Generally, you'll have to pay   e for a permit; often, the fee is based n the projected value of the impro ement. When applying for your permit, be as accurate as possible about the improvement's projected cost; overestimating its value may push the fee higher.

Zoning ordinances restrict the height of residential buildings, limit lot cov-

erage (the amount of the lot a building or group of buildings may cover), specify setbacks (how close to the property lines you can build), and, in some areas, stipulate architectural design standards.

Though overheads, gazebos, and other garden structures rarely exceed height limitations, they often are affected by setback requirements (see illustration below). These structures also add to your overall lot coverage, an important concern if you anticipate adding on to your home in the future.

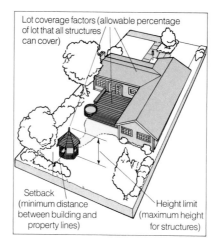

Lot coverage factors (allowable percentage of lot that all structures can cover)

Setback (minimum distance between building and property lines)

Height limit (maximum height for structures)

In some neighborhoods, your improvement may have to meet certain architectural standards. If so, your plans must go before an architectural review board, dramatically increasing the time it takes to get your project moving.

Property deeds can also restrict a project's design, construction, or location. Check your deed for easements, architectural-standard restrictions, or other limitations.

DRAWING UP A DESIGN

Though most of the projects in this book were designed and built to blend into a very specific setting, you may be able to modify them to suit your particular needs. For complicated alterations, consider getting some design help.

Even if you're planning to turn the project over to a professional, it's more efficient and less costly if you can work up a preliminary plan or design beforehand.

A good scale drawing will show you how well your roof design is working and how it fits into the house-garden relationship. If you're planning a gazebo or detached garden structure, the drawing will enable you to visualize logical traffic patterns, relative size and shape, and location.

Making a base map. Use graph paper to make a base map that shows the physical properties of your lot and house. (If you can locate architect's drawings or deed maps that show the actual dimensions and orientation of your property, you'll save hours of complicated measuring and drawing.)

Be sure to show the following on your base map:
● Dimensions of your lot
● Location of the house, pool, spa, and other structures
● Doors and windows and the rooms from which they open
● Points of the compass
● Path and direction of the sun and any hot spots it may create
● Utilities (water, gas, and sewer lines) and the depth of each; underground wires
● Setback lines
● Direction of the prevailing winds
● Existing trees and large plants
● Any obstructions beyond the lot that may affect sun, view, or privacy

Experimenting with your ideas. On your base map, analyze the best site for your overhead. Next, place tracing paper over your map and sketch your ideal roof design. Then, with a scale ruler, calculate what its actual dimensions would be. Go out to the yard and confirm its size and placement, using a tape measure.

Now you're ready to consider the style of structure that appeals to you. For help, study the patio roof and gazebo designs that appear throughout this book. As you design your own structure, remember to take into account allowable beam and rafter spans (see the chart on page 76).

WORKING WITH PROFESSIONALS

Many people adding an overhead or other garden structure seek some professional help at either the design or the construction stage of their project.

Some homeowners rely on professionals to design the structure, draw up plans, and supervise construction. Others hire someone to see that the work gets done. Still others act as their own contractor.

To find design professionals or builders, ask friends or neighbors who have had similar work done. Trade associations can recommend licensed professionals in your area.

If you're adding a gazebo, there are gazebo builders who offer stock designs which they will customize to your specifications. Gazebos are also available in kit form (see pages 60–61).

Design & Building Professionals

Here are some of the professionals who can help you, along with suggestions for working with them.

Architects and landscape architects are state-licensed professionals with degrees in architecture or landscape architecture. They're trained to create designs that are structurally sound, functional, and aesthetically pleasing. They also know construction materials, can negotiate bids from contractors, and can supervise the actual work.

Landscape and building designers usually have a landscape architect's education and training but are not licensed. Building designers may offer design help along with construction.

Draftspersons make the working drawings which are required before you can secure building permits, drawings from which you or your contractor can work.

They also may design structures with wood-frame construction. For modifying plans in this book, a qualified draftsperson may be your best choice.

Soils and structural engineers need to be consulted if you're planning to build a structure on an unstable or steep lot or where heavy wind or loads may come into play.

Soils engineers evaluate soil conditions on a proposed construction site and establish design specifications for foundations that can resist whatever stresses unstable soil exerts.

Structural engineers, often working with the calculations a soils engineer provides, design foundation piers and footings to suit the site. They also may provide wind- and load-stress calculations as required.

General and landscape contractors specialize in construction (garden construction in the case of landscape contractors), though some also have design skills and experience as well. Contractors may do all the work themselves, or they may assume responsibility for hiring qualified subcontractors, ordering construction materials, and seeing that the job is completed according to contract.

Subcontractors will have to be hired and supervised if you act as your own general contractor. You'll be responsible for permits, insurance, and payroll taxes, as well as direct supervision of all the aspects of construction.

When dealing with subcontractors, give them clear instructions, put all agreements in writing, and provide as much direct supervision as you can.

The Design Process

At least three different working arrangements are open to you if you choose to work with an architect or landscape architect.

Retained on a consultation basis, an architect or landscape architect will review your plans, possibly suggest ideas for a more effective design, and perhaps provide a couple of rough con-

ceptual sketches. Then it will be up to you to do the working drawings.

Another route is to hire a professional to design or modify your project and provide working drawings, with the understanding that you will take responsibility for overseeing construction.

Last, you can retain an architect or landscape architect on a planning-through-construction basis. Besides designing your project and providing working drawings and specifications, the architect will draw up bid forms, negotiate bids, arrange contracts with general contractors or subcontractors, check on materials, and supervise construction.

Working this way will cost you more (usually 10 to 15 percent of the cost of the work), but you'll be free from the plethora of details you would otherwise have to handle.

If you hire an architect or landscape architect, here is the process you can expect.

Initial planning. First, you and your architect will meet together to begin planning the project. Any materials you can give the architect—your preliminary sketches, blueprints of your house, deed maps, and photographs of structures you like—can streamline the process and may save you money. In this meeting, you will also discuss fee, method of payment, and responsibilities.

When you receive the architect's bid, be sure it's specific on all of those points. Will the architect do all necessary survey work and deal with the building department? How will suggestions for design changes be handled? Will any outside consultants—such as a soils engineer—be needed, and, if so, who will pay them? Who will bid out the job to contractors and oversee construction?

The working drawings. With your input and approval, the architect will develop working drawings. Typically, these cover construction details, planting design, site considerations, and plans for irrigation or electrical work. To receive a building permit, you may need a site plan (showing your property and the structures on it, along with the planned structures), a plan view of new structures, elevation views, and important details.

Construction bids. Once the plans are complete, the design firm asks for bids from contractors (usually at least three). To be sure the bids are competitive, you may want to consider getting a few bids on your own.

You are under no obligation to choose the contractor who gives you the lowest bid. Base your decision on both the individual's reputation (check references carefully) and the bid. Be sure the contractor is someone you feel comfortable with. The person you select should be well established, cooperative, competent, and financially solvent.

Writing a Contract

If you hire a contractor to build your garden structure, you'll need a written contract. The more complete your contract, the better the chance that neither the process nor the result will be flawed. It's a good idea to consult a lawyer before signing any agreement for work on your property. If any differences arise, you should be able to refer to the contract to help resolve the problem.

Here are some items you can expect to find in the contract:

■ *Construction materials* should be identified by brand name, quality markings (species, grades, and other quality identifiers), and model numbers where applicable. Anything not included and added later will increase your costs.

■ *Work to be performed* should be clearly stated in the contract. If, for example, you want the contractor to prepare the site, the contract should explicitly identify appropriate tasks: remove fences and shrubs, tear out concrete, grade, and so forth.

■ *A time schedule* for the project—a beginning date and a completion date—may be stipulated in your contract. The contractor obviously cannot be responsible for construction delays caused by strikes and material shortages. Still, you want the job completed within a reasonable period of time. Your best leverage is a good working relationship with the contractor, as well as the stipulation that the final payment will be withheld until work is completed.

■ *The method of payment* is also covered in the contract. Either one payment is made at the beginning and the balance upon completion of the project, or payment is made in installments as work progresses.

SELECTING MATERIALS

Most outdoor structures, whether they're gazebos, patio roofs, arbors, pergolas, or some other similar overhead, are built from wood. Generally, the posts, beams, and rafters are made from boards or dimension lumber; the roof may be constructed from boards, lath or battens, or woven wood.

But your choices aren't limited to wood. Other popular materials for roofs are outdoor fabrics, plastic or glass panels, screening, and such solid roofing materials as asphalt shingles or roll roofing. Posts can be made from concrete or steel, as well as wood.

The information that follows will help you sort out the possibilities and choose a material that's appropriate for your needs. To learn how to work with each material, turn to the techniques chapter beginning on page 70.

Wood—for Style & Substance

The most popular material for patio roof structures, gazebos, and other overheads is wood. It's easy to cut, shape, and fabricate; it comes in a wide range of sizes, from thin lath to large beams; and it offers a variety of species, grades, and textures. Probably most importantly, wood has a natural appearance that looks good outdoors.

For complete information on buying lumber, see the "Lumber Buyers Guide" on page 71.

One of the traits that makes wood so popular for outdoor structures is the way it reflects nature's beauty. Landscape architect: Thomas L. Berger Associates.

Lumber sizes. Narrow lumber (up to ¾ inch thick) is commonly referred to as either *lath* or *batten*. The word *boards* generally denotes lumber that's ¾ or 1 inch thick and more than 2 inches wide. Lumber that's between 2 and 4 inches thick and is at least 2 inches wide is called *dimension lumber*. *Timber* is anything larger.

■ *Lath* is sometimes used for open-style roofing. Strictly speaking, common outdoor lath is rough-surfaced redwood or cedar that's about ⅜ inch by 1½ inches; it's sold in lengths of 4, 6, and 8 feet, often in bundles of 50. In a broader sense, the term "lath" can refer to any open-work slat roofing where lengths run parallel.

For outdoor overheads, look for high-quality lath that's free of excessive knots or other defects. Relatively straight grain is also important to minimize the warping and twisting that can occur under constantly changing weather conditions.

■ *Batten* resembles overgrown lath, milled in thicknesses of ¼ to ¾ inch and in widths of 2 to 3 inches. Batten can be purchased in lengths up to 20 feet and is generally sold by the piece. Though smooth-surfaced batten is sometimes called lattice, it's not sold under this name in all localities. (The term "lattice" is also used to describe a cross-hatch panel.)

■ *Boards, dimension lumber, and timber* are the most commonly used materials for posts, beams, rafters, and open-style roofing. Throughout this book, you'll see 1 by 2s, 2 by 4s, 4 by 4s, and other typical sizes used again and again in the projects, in many different combinations and configurations.

Lumber textures. When lumber is milled, several different textures can be produced. Though surfaced lumber—smooth on all four sides—is the most familiar, rough or resawn textures are often favored for a more rustic look.

■ *Surfaced lumber*, the type generally available in lumberyards and home-improvement centers, has been planed smooth on all four sides (designated "S4S"); you can also get it planed on only one, two, or three sides. It's suited to all types of outdoor construction and can be stained or painted.

Note that the actual sizes of surfaced boards and dimension lumber are less than those suggested by their names, as shown below. The difference is the amount removed in the planing process.

STANDARD DIMENSIONS OF SOFTWOODS

Nominal size	Surfaced (actual) size
1 by 1	¾″ by ¾″
1 by 2	¾″ by 1½″
1 by 3	¾″ by 2½″
1 by 4	¾″ by 3½″
1 by 6	¾″ by 5½″
1 by 8	¾″ by 7¼″
1 by 10	¾″ by 9¼″
1 by 12	¾″ by 11¼″
2 by 2	1½″ by 1½″
2 by 3	1½″ by 2½″
2 by 4	1½″ by 3½″
2 by 6	1½″ by 5½″
2 by 8	1½″ by 7¼″
2 by 10	1½″ by 9¼″
2 by 12	1½″ by 11¼″
4 by 4	3½″ by 3½″
4 by 6	3½″ by 5½″
4 by 8	3½″ by 7¼″
4 by 10	3½″ by 9¼″
4 by 12	3½″ by 11¼″

■ *Rough lumber* has been milled but not planed. Its surfaces are rough and splintery, and it usually has a higher moisture content than surfaced lumber. Though rough lumber can be used to achieve a very rustic look, its splintery texture makes it unfriendly to touch. It can be stained but is a poor surface for painting.

Buying rough lumber can save you money, but shop carefully: pieces with excessive knots, flat grain, or too high a moisture content can warp and twist, aging prematurely.

■ *Resawn lumber* is preferred by many landscape professionals because of its rustic, but not too rough, texture. Though rough lumber is generally available only in the lowest grades, any grade can be resawn—a benefit where higher grades are needed for strength. Additionally, resawn lumber takes a stain beautifully. Generally, it must be special-ordered.

■ *Sandblasted lumber* isn't really a milled product, but it has a rustic appearance similar to resawn wood. Sandblasting surfaced lumber is generally not cost-effective unless you're having other sandblasting work done (on your pool or siding, for example).

Lesser-known wood products. Though they don't fit into standard lumber categories, several other wood products are commonly used in the construction of outdoor overheads. Some are readily available; others require more searching.

■ *Stakes and poles*, available at garden and lumber supply outlets, can be used for rustic, open-style roofing. Grapestakes, favorites of fence-builders, offer

Rustic tree-stake overhead provides some shade, supports leafy vine. Landscape design: G. Grisamore Design, Inc.

Crisp, white lattice panels on overhead shade small brick patio outside back door; used on cornice and wide posts, they lend an air of formality to house and garden. Landscape architect: Bill Derringer.

a hand-hewn look. Made from redwood or cedar, grapestakes are roughly 2 by 2 inches and are usually available in 6-foot lengths. Split grapestakes, more the size of 1 by 2s, also make a satisfactory, rustic-looking cover.

■ *Peeler cores*, a by-product of plywood manufacturing, are rustic, inexpensive landscape timbers that may be used for non-structural purposes. They come round or with two flat sides and are typically about 6 inches in diameter and 8 feet long. Though most have been pressure-treated with preservatives, this treatment may offer only minimal decay protection. They don't take a finish well, and tend to warp.

■ *Bean poles, lodgepoles, and tree stakes* are additional products you may be able to find. Bean poles, 1- by 1-inch lengths of redwood or cedar, and preservative-treated lodgepoles and tree stakes lend a very rustic appearance to an overhead. Some specialty landscape supply firms sell treated lodgepoles up to 12 inches in diameter.

Reed, bamboo, and other woven woods.
These woods, natives of the South Pacific and Orient, may be a good choice where you want to achieve an Oriental motif. They're inexpensive, lightweight, and easy to handle. However, most are not very durable.

■ *Woven reed* comes in 15- and 25-foot rolls that measure 6 feet wide. The reed is woven with a stainless steel wire to help withstand the elements. The wire can be easily cut and retwisted when the roll is being trimmed to the dimensions of the overhead, but the stiffness of the wire keeps the woven reed from being freely adjustable in an overhead screen.

Since constant flexing of the wire strands causes them to fail quickly, nail or staple the material to a rigid frame.

Available at many nurseries and garden supply centers, reed rolls will last several seasons, especially if they can be removed and brought under cover during the rainy season.

■ *Woven bamboo*, which is manufactured primarily for vertical shade use, comes in rolls that vary in width from 3 to 12 feet; standard length is 6 feet. It's available in wired form, similar to reed.

There are two main grades: split and matchstick. Split bamboo is coarser and less regular than matchstick, which is made from thin strips of the inner layer of the bamboo stalk. Price varies depending on quality.

The split type is preferable for most installations since it's stiffer than matchstick. For an adjustable overhead suspended from wires, however, matchstick bamboo is often used because of its flexibility.

■ *Woven spruce and basswood* are similar to woven bamboo. They're generally woven with string, but because the wood shade is made specifically for outdoor use, a high grade of seine twine is used. The twine will probably last as long as any cotton cord.

Preassembled lattice panels.
These panels offer the look of lattice—crisscrossed lath—without the work of measuring, cutting, and fastening each piece individually.

Wood lattice panels are manufactured in 4- by 8-foot, 2- by 8-foot, and 4- by 6-foot sizes. Several grades are available, depending on the quality, thickness, and spacing of the wood lath and the care taken in manufacturing. Only redwood and cedar panels are durable enough for outdoor use. Patterns vary: you can buy diagonal or checkerboard designs, or variations on these themes.

Another type of lattice panel you can buy is made not from wood but from PVC (vinyl). Resembling carefully painted wood lattice, vinyl panels are smooth, very tough, and never require refinishing. They're also more expensive than wood.

Vinyl panels are available in white and several earth tones. Typical sheet sizes are 4 by 8 feet and 2 feet 10 inches by 8 feet. You can buy panels with diagonal or rectangular lath patterns of different weights and lath spacings.

Outdoor Fabrics: Colorful Protection

Colorful and water-resistant, canvas and similar fabrics are favored by many for awnings and patio roofs. These fabrics can block or diffuse sun, shed rain, and add color and texture to a home or garden. The nature of the different materials allows them to be drawn taut into flat planes, to curve gracefully over vaulted skeletons, or to hang and gather like curtains.

Because fabrics are lightweight, the supporting structures needn't look massive (though large expanses exposed to wind may require an engineered framing). Many canvas-style covers also offer versatility—they can be rolled up or folded away when not needed.

Because they're so visible in the landscape but must withstand the rigors of rain, wind, sun, and snow, most awning materials combine the attractiveness of a home-furnishing fabric with the durability of an industrial one. Whether made from a natural or synthetic fiber, the fabric should retain its color and last at least 4 years.

The specialty fabrics discussed below are generally found at awning and shade stores. Look through samples for the colors, patterns, and properties that are right for your application. Keep in mind that manufacturers are continually improving these materials and introducing new ones to the market.

Also, you might consider other kinds of outdoor fabrics, such as those used for tents, sails, and other sporting goods. Be sure you know the advantages—and disadvantages—of the fabric you choose. For example, ripstop nylon occasionally finds use in overheads, but it's not as strong as the other outdoor fabrics and is prone to sun damage.

Acrylic fabrics. Until recently, painted, fungus-proofed Army duck canvas was the most practical of the outdoor fabrics. Now, acrylic fabrics have edged canvas out of the top spot for awnings and fabric patio covers.

Though acrylics are priced competitively with canvas, they're nearly twice as durable. They're also colorfast, mildew-resistant, and much more apt to stretch than tear. In addition, they'll shed the rain without leaking. (However, if they're "bagged" with a puddle of water, poking a broom handle against them will usually cause them to drip.)

The manmade fiber, which should last 5 to 10 years, has a soft, woven look and is offered in a broad palette of colors and patterns. These fabrics are translucent, though the degree of translucency varies with color. On the negative side, the fabrics are woven, so colors may not be as crisp as colors painted on cotton duck.

Under normal conditions, acrylics won't mildew, unless leaves and debris are left to mildew on top of them. (Occasional hosing accompanied by a light brushing to remove dirt, leaves, and twigs will help prolong the fabric's life and maintain its beauty.)

Weight is typically 8½ ounces per square yard; fabric width is normally 46 inches, though 60-inch fabrics are available in some marine grades.

Painted or dyed cotton duck (canvas). Cotton duck comes in a variety of solid colors or stripes. The painted type has a coat of acrylic paint on its outer (weather-facing) surface. The paint, which has a dull finish, leaves the linen texture visible; from the underside, you see a pearl green (sometimes patterned) surface. Because of the layer of paint, the duck is opaque. With normal maintenance, it should last 5 to 8 years.

Dyed duck has color running throughout the fabric. It can be waterproofed to extend its life, but generally, it won't last as long as the acrylic-painted duck.

Because duck is a natural fabric, it's more prone to mildew than the acrylic type. Also, the painted fabric may become brittle with time.

Vinyl-coated cotton canvas. The shiny outside surface of this fabric shows little or no texture. Available in solid colors or striped (usually white with a primary color), it weathers and cleans well.

Gazebo roofed with acrylic fabric nestles in corner of deck; simple framework consists of 4 by 4 posts, 4 by 6 beams, and 4 by 4 rafters. Architect: James Oliver.

The opaque, green-colored underside keeps the area beneath cool and shaded. Its life span is 4 to 7 years.

Vinyl-laminated polyester. This fabric sandwiches an open-weave polyester scrim between two layers of painted vinyl. The scrim allows light to pass through, making the area below brighter and warmer than with a solid fabric. Sold in a wide range of solid colors and stripes, the fabric's underside may be either colored or sand white. The surface has a mat finish. Good in humid areas, the material should last 5 to 8 years.

Though the scrim is very strong, the vinyl can delaminate if repeatedly folded.

Screening Materials

Screening filters sunlight and, when fine meshes are used, also repels insects and pests. A wide array of screening materials is available today. The most popular types are made from aluminum or fiberglass.

Though your local hardware or home-improvement store may not stock all the different types, you can probably find out where to purchase the one you want. Or check the Yellow Pages under "Screens—Door & Window."

Aluminum screening. Corrosion-resistant aluminum screening has a long life expectancy under normal conditions; however, like other metals, it will deteriorate in coastal or industrial atmospheres. While not as strong as galvanized steel, it tends to bulge if struck or strained rather than to break, as steel will. In weight, it's the lightest of the metals.

Vinyl-coated fiberglass. Strong and lightweight, vinyl-coated fiberglass won't corrode or oxidize. Because it doesn't stretch, it can cover larger panels than other types of screening. It's available in widths up to 84 inches.

Plastic mesh. One of the best screening materials for houses located in coastal areas, plastic mesh will not corrode and is unaffected by humidity or salt air. Available by the running foot in widths of 24, 30, 36, 42, and 48 inches (some types go up to 6 feet), plastic mesh can be ordered by the roll or by the piece. Be aware that wider widths may be difficult to pull tight and nail, and they may tend to sag.

Aluminum-and-plastic screening. The horizontal wires of this screening hybrid are broad and flat, reducing sun penetration and resulting in lower inside temperatures. Colored a neutral gray, the screen is easy to see through from the inside, yet affords daytime privacy. Wires are plastic-coated.

Greenhouse shadecloth. Depending on its weave, shadecloth blocks sunlight to varying degrees—you buy it by the percentage of light it blocks. The synthetic screening takes grommets and holds up well when exposed to harsh weather and sun. It also can be sewn. Because it's plastic, it won't rust or corrode.

Standard widths range from 28 to 48 inches; special weaves run up to 20-foot widths and 900-foot lengths. Since it may shrink about 2 percent during the first 2 months of exposure to hot sunlight, shadecloth should be installed loose.

Plastic & Glass for Shelter, Light

Plastic or glass used in skylights or as a solid roofing material can provide protection from rain and still allow plenty of light to penetrate. Used in a well-conceived design, these transparent or translucent materials can maximize light, view, and shelter in an outdoor room.

When used improperly, however, a plastic or glass roof can act as a heat trap or create a condensation and drip prob-

Molded acrylic roof panels form an impressive greenhouse enjoyed by plants and people alike. During winter, glass panels can be added to sides to enclose space completely. Architect: John Storrs.

lem, making life beneath it miserable. Why? Though plastic and glass will let radiant heat in, heated or moisture-laden air can't get out, so heat builds up and the moisture in warmed air condenses on the cool plastic or glass surfaces.

Acrylic plastic. Acrylic is shatter-resistant, weighs less than glass, and can be transparent or translucent—ideal traits for a roofing material where rain repellency and light transmission are important. In addition, sheets of acrylic are easy to cut, drill, and fasten with fairly standard woodworking tools. (They can even be shaped or curved on the job site.)

Cast acrylic, used as a skylight material, has the best weathering record of the nonglass skylight glazing materials.

On the negative side, acrylic scratches easily. Because of this, you may want to limit its use to areas where scratches are unlikely to occur (away from trees, for example) or where they will go unnoticed.

You can buy transparent, translucent, or even opaque acrylic plastic in almost every color or tint in the rainbow, though clear is the most commonly used. Remember that any color will shed the same color light on the surfaces beneath it.

Thicknesses range from $\frac{1}{8}$ to $\frac{1}{2}$ inch. The most commonly used are $\frac{1}{8}$, $\frac{3}{16}$, and $\frac{1}{4}$ inch. Of course, the thicker the material, the more expensive it is, but thin materials require more support to prevent sagging and are more likely to crack.

To find acrylic plastic dealers, look under "Plastics—Rods, Tubes, Sheets, Etc." in the Yellow Pages.

Polycarbonate plastic and fiberglass.

Often used in skylight glazing, these materials are more impact-resistant than acrylic, but they don't weather as well. Both materials may begin to yellow after about 5 years, eventually affecting light transmission. Some of the yellowing of polycarbonates can be removed by washing the skylight annually with approved detergents.

Clear spa roof is made from 4 by 8 acrylic panels fastened to a simple wooden frame. Bamboo screen adds privacy. Design: Katsu Hirasawa.

Some skylight manufacturers combine acrylic with fiberglass to give the glazing the impact resistance of fiberglass and the weathering quality of acrylic.

Polyester resin and vinyl. These widely used patio-roofing materials are often reinforced with fiberglass for added strength. Some polyester panels include fiberglass matting and, for long life, a coating of acrylic resin (chemically bonded). An adequate coating will protect panels for up to 10 years.

Translucent types are the most popular. You can choose from several patterns: corrugated, flat, crimped, staggered shiplap, or simulated board-and-batten. Corrugated opaque vinyl panels are also available; these block the light entirely (some designers alternate them with translucent panels).

A related plastic, polyethylene, is available in sheets from .0015 to .020 inch thick. Polyethylene makes a very inexpensive cover material, but it only lasts a season or two.

Standard panel sizes range from 24 to $50\frac{1}{2}$ inches in width and 8 to 20 feet in length. Thickness varies by color and

type. Corrugated rolls run 40 inches wide; flat rolls are 36 inches wide. If you design your patio roof using the standard sizes sold by most dealers, construction will usually be easier, since construction accessories are manufactured for standard-size panels.

Though these plastics come in a broad spectrum of colors, be very careful in selecting one for a patio overhead. Remember that the plastic will color the light on your patio, and perhaps even a window wall of your house. It will also affect the temperature on your patio: if you live in a hot climate, you'll want to pick a light, reflective color.

Glass. Because glass is relatively expensive, quite heavy and fragile, and very tricky to work with, it's best to consult a design professional if you want to use it. The structure will need to support the glass effectively and allow for the proper control of heat and moisture.

A professional can help you choose the right glass for the job—there's a confusing array available. For example, you can use energy-efficient insulating glass for an enclosed greenhouse-type space. Or you can get tinted and coated glass to reduce the amount of light, glare, and heat from the sun.

Be advised that in nearly all overhead applications, building codes closely regulate both the acceptable types of glass and the supporting framework. For safety, tempered, laminated, or wire-reinforced glass should be used.

Solid Roofing Materials

If you're planning a solid-roofed overhead or gazebo, you'll want the roofing material to blend with the one used on your house. Also, be sure to consider roof pitch, or slope, when designing a solid roof. (See the section on solid roofing beginning on page 85 for information on the correct roof pitch for each roofing material.)

Typical choices for solid roofing are described below.

Asphalt shingles are economical, easy to install and maintain, and widely available in a broad range of colors, shapes, and specialty patterns. They typically measure 12 by 36 inches.

Wood shingles and shakes, typically made from western red cedar, offer natural beauty and durability. Shingles, with their smooth, finished appearance, are available in 16-, 18-, and 24-inch lengths. The thicker shakes, roughly split by machine or by hand, come in 18- or 24-inch lengths. You can buy them in two weights, medium and heavy, and in several styles.

Though several grades are available, heartwood-grade shakes are the most durable.

Sidings aren't meant to be used as watertight, finished roofing materials, but they can provide serviceable roofing for gazebos and similar structures when pitched for water runoff.

■ *Solid-board sidings* are milled in a variety of patterns. Most appropriate for roofing are horizontal shiplap or bevel patterns that shed rain like shingles. You'll need to use building paper underneath for rain protection. Some localities also require a layer of sheathing (check with your building department).

Solid-board siding is available in several species; redwood and cedar are the most popular because of their natural resistance to decay. Boards are generally an inch thick; widths vary from 4 to 12 inches, and lengths run up to 20 feet.

Sold either finished or unfinished, untreated solid-board siding must be finished to withstand the elements (see page 94).

■ *Plywood and hardboard sidings* can serve as both sheathing and siding. They come in either sheets, which cover a large surface quickly, or lap boards, which are like board siding.

Standard sheet sizes are 4 feet wide by 8 to 10 feet long. Lap boards are 6 to 12 inches wide and 16 feet long. Thicknesses range from $\frac{3}{8}$ to $\frac{5}{8}$ inch.

Typical species for these types of sidings are Douglas fir, western red cedar, southern pine, and redwood. Siding plywood is sold finished or unfinished; untreated types must be finished.

■ *Vinyl and aluminum sidings,* man-made materials, are used in the same way as board siding. They won't rot, rust, or blister, but vinyl can fade and aluminum dents easily. No finishing is required.

Patterns simulate board siding. Widths vary; standard length is $12\frac{1}{2}$ feet. Aluminum is also sold in 36- or 48-inch panels 12 inches wide in a pattern that resembles cedar shakes.

Asphalt roll roofing is probably the fastest roofing material to install. Commonly used on very shallowly pitched

Graceful shingle-roofed overhead offers cool garden oasis sheltered from hot sun.

Tile roofing, though elegant, requires construction expertise. Landscape architect: Fry + Stone Associates.

roofs, it's available in a variety of colors. Roll roofing comes in 36-inch-wide, 36-foot-long rolls.

Clay and concrete tiles come in several shapes and in a wide spectrum of colors, from subtle earth tones to blue, yellow, and red. Typically, they measure 12 by 17 inches and are ½ inch thick. These materials, very durable and attractive-looking, generally require professional installation.

Weight is the most critical factor if you're considering roofing with tile. Tiles weigh 900 to 1,000 pounds per square (100 square feet)—three to four times as much as asphalt shingles—and your roof and its supporting structure must be sturdy enough to handle the load.

Aluminum panels are occasionally used for outdoor roofing. Aluminum is sold as a do-it-yourself product at building supply outlets. An excellent material for outdoor construction, it can't rust, rot, or warp. In addition, it's lightweight, easy to handle, workable with standard woodworking tools, and economical. Aluminum paneling also sheds water and snow well.

On the negative side, it can corrode, bend, and dent, and it can sound like an oversize snare drum in a rainstorm.

Aluminum panels are excellent for reflecting heat in the daytime. At night or on cool days, they can reflect interior warmth back into the patio area.

Panels are available smooth or in embossed patterns. Besides the conventional corrugation, there are V-crimp and "flat-top" rib configurations. You may choose from several colors.

The panels come in widths that will give a 24-inch coverage with lap. Colored panels come in lengths of 8, 10, 12, 14, and 16 feet; plain ones vary from 6 to 24 feet.

Aluminum shingles, shaped to interlock with each other for good wind resistance, are sometimes preferred in areas of heavy snow because of their durability. Often corrugated, they come

Sculptured stucco column supports open patio roof (see page 25 for another view). Landscape architect: Forsum/Summers & Partners.

in various colors. They're lightweight and relatively easy to handle.

Built-up roofing systems, for flat or low-sloping roofs, may have surfaces of either asphalt and gravel or polyurethane foam. Asphalt, or tar, and gravel roofs are made from several layers of roofing felt, each coated with hot- or cold-mopped asphalt. The uppermost layer is then surfaced with crushed rock or gravel. Obviously, this must be done by a professional.

Materials for Posts

Though wood posts are standard for most patio roofs and gazebos, concrete, steel, and other materials are occasionally used in special situations—to provide exceptional strength or to blend with the design of the house, for example.

Concrete and stucco columns. In some designs, posts made from concrete or stuccoed framework support patio overheads. Square or rectangular concrete columns are made the traditional way—concrete is poured into wood forms. Cylindrical fiber tubes are used to form round columns. Stucco columns, such as

Spare but strong, steel posts provide a framework for an acrylic fabric roof. Landscape architect: Fry + Stone Associates.

the one shown above, at left, are constructed from concrete blocks or wood frames, which are then stuccoed.

As a rule, masonry work is expensive and requires careful engineering.

Steel structures. Impervious to fire, rot, and termite hazards, steel posts offer exceptional strength in small dimensions; they're good for strong, uncluttered substructures. Often, steel posts are hidden under a facade of wood, thus eliminating the need for knee braces and increasing overall strength.

Because structural steel is a costly substructure material, it's often reserved for use where extreme loads must be carried over unstable soil.

Most steel structures must be professionally engineered. In addition, flanges for attaching the post to the pier and beam must be welded to the ends, and the posts must be cut to length. This requires extra care when installing concrete piers and estimating post heights—steel posts cannot be adjusted on the job. They must be painted periodically for protection against rust.

If you're considering a steel structure, consult an architect or engineer on its design and construction. For materials, check welding shops in your area.

PATIO ROOFS

Wind, rain, and sun shouldn't deter your enjoyment of the great outdoors. Turn Mother Nature into an ally, not an enemy, with a well-designed, carefully situated patio roof. On a hot day, it can transform a scorching patio or deck into an oasis from the heat. In a wet climate, an overhead can block wind and rain, allowing you to entertain and relax outdoors when the weather would otherwise drive you inside.

In this section we present a variety of patio roofs and other overheads, and show how they were constructed. Let them spark your imagination and creativity as you design your own roof. In most cases, you'll need to adapt the plans to fit your particular setting.

At home in a natural setting, two-tiered overhead shades patio beneath and offers plenty of visual interest in this comprehensive garden design.

TWO-TIERED GARDEN ROOF

Round posts stand like trees to support this two-level, shade-casting patio roof (shown on facing page). Six-inch-diameter treated lodgepoles, purchased from a specialty landscape supplier, give this structure its natural, yet distinctive, character.

To cut a lodgepole, you can use a circular saw, rolling the pole as you cut (if necessary, finish the cuts with a handsaw). The ends are chamfered to refine their appearance—for this, use a circular saw or a plane.

Doubled 2 by 10 and 2 by 12 beams sandwiching the posts interlock so effectively that they eliminate the need for cross bracing (be sure to have a similar structure professionally engineered).

You'll have to drill through the beams first, using one to mark and drill its mate. Then hold each beam in place to serve as a pattern for marking the lodgepoles. Remove the beam and drill through the poles (you may need an extension shaft for the drill bit).

The lengths of 3 by 3 lumber that make up the open-style roof and the resawn beams (all Douglas fir) were special-ordered. All the lumber was lightly sandblasted and stained before assembly.

Landscape architect: Forsum/Summers & Partners.

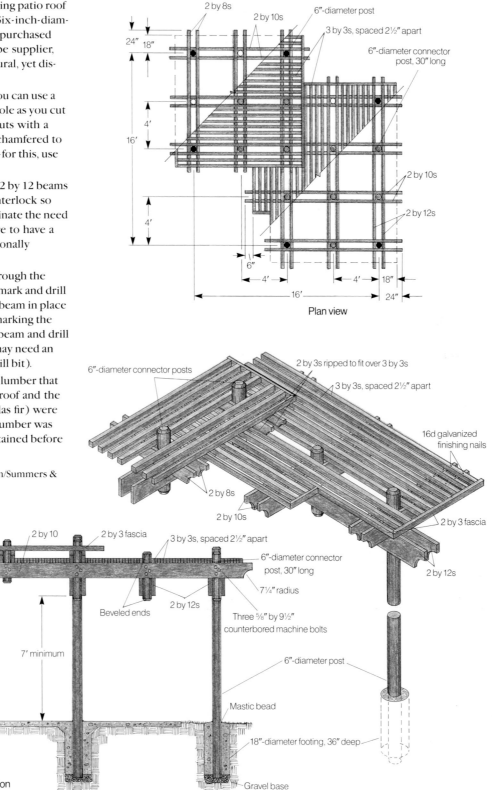

Plan view

Elevation

POOLSIDE PAVILION

A solid, rectilinear frame supports the lattice panels of this shady poolside retreat. Though the structure is of basic post-and-beam construction, 2 by 4s nailed to its posts and beams beef it up and lend it a stagelike appearance. The latticework extensions give it a strong, substantial look. Cross braces work both as decorative accents and as all-important structural members.

Long spans overhead provide a large open area below. The framework is made from Douglas fir; posts are held slightly above ground level by post anchors. Post bottoms are sealed to prevent moisture penetration. The prefabricated lattice panels, kept to a maximum of about 3 feet square to prevent warping, are stapled at each intersection.

The easiest way to finish such a structure is to spray on an opaque stain before construction.

Landscape architect: John J. Greenwood & Associates, Inc.

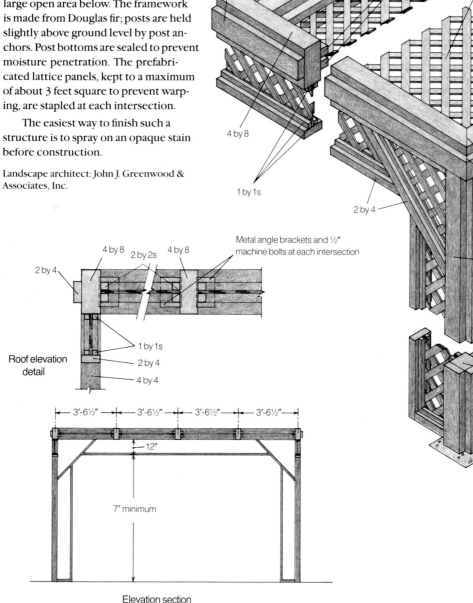

2 by 4 nailed flat around perimeter

4 by 8

2 by 2 supports above and below lattice

Prefabricated lattice panels, cut to fit

4 by 8

1 by 1s

Mitered corners

2 by 4

2 by 4s

4 by 4

Metal angle brackets and ½″ machine bolts at each intersection

4 by 8   2 by 2s   4 by 8

2 by 4

1 by 1s

2 by 4

Roof elevation detail

4 by 4

Anchored to footing as required by code

3′-6½″   3′-6½″   3′-6½″   3′-6½″

12″

7′ minimum

Elevation section

**Prefabricated lattice panels, set into a
bold framework, dapple sunshine for
comfortable poolside enjoyment.**

■Bold Sun Shelter

Extending from this home's west-facing side, this sound overhead provides both a feeling of enclosure and an escape from the heat and glare of the strong afternoon sun.

Doubled 3 by 8 beams running parallel to the house are bolted to the sides of the posts. From a 2 by 8 ledger lagscrewed to the house wall, doubled 4 by 8 beams hang from short connector posts. Shade is thrown by 2 by 4s on edge, spaced 6 inches center to center. Because the overhead is attached to the house, cross bracing isn't necessary.

Posts are built out with 2 by 4s on each face. To soften the lines, beam and post edges are beveled with a router. To drill through the full thicknesses of beams and posts, either toenail the beams in place and drill through them with a drill bit on an extension shaft, or measure and predrill matching holes before lifting the beams into place.

Landscape architect: John J. Greenwood & Associates, Inc.

Facing Pacific Ocean, deep and wide overhead with simple, uncluttered lines throws shade on both patio and house until sun melts into horizon.

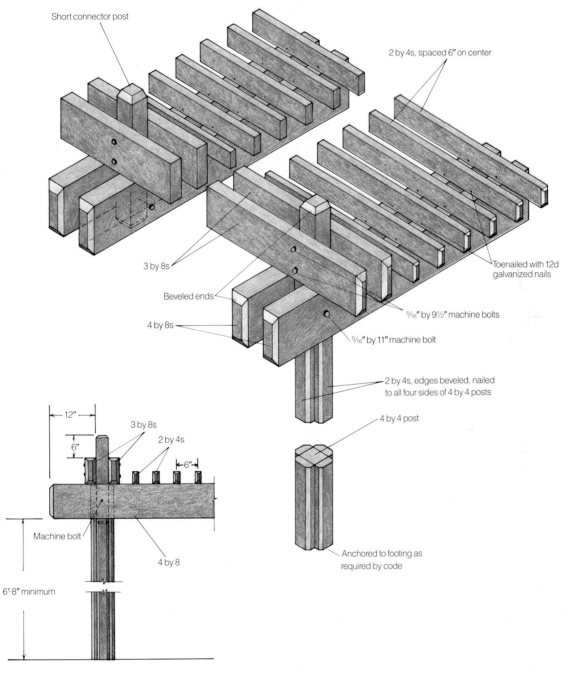

Short connector post

2 by 4s, spaced 6" on center

3 by 8s

Beveled ends

4 by 8s

Toenailed with 12d galvanized nails

⁵⁄₁₆" by 9½" machine bolts

⁵⁄₁₆" by 11" machine bolt

2 by 4s, edges beveled, nailed to all four sides of 4 by 4 posts

4 by 4 post

Anchored to footing as required by code

12"

3 by 8s

6"

2 by 4s

6"

Machine bolt

4 by 8

6'-8" minimum

Elevation

■STUCCOED-COLUMN OVERHEADS

Stuccoed columns supporting an overhead declare durability and strength. Though the large beams on the overheads shown here and on the facing page offer little actual cover, both structures define the space below with authority.

In each case, the columns are built from concrete blocks that are filled with mortar and reinforced with steel bars. Building stuccoed columns is a job best left to a professional mason unless you're well-versed in masonry skills.

More form than function, heavy 6 by 12 beams topped with 6 by 8s—all routed, sandblasted, and stained white—are anchored to sturdy, stuccoed concrete-block columns. Landscape architect: Nick Williams.

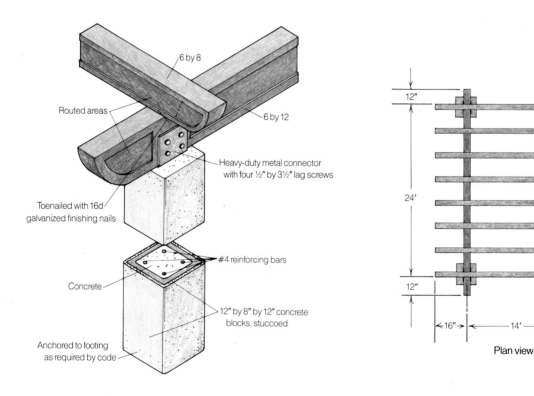

6 by 8

Routed areas

6 by 12

Heavy-duty metal connector with four ½" by 3½" lag screws

Toenailed with 16d galvanized finishing nails

#4 reinforcing bars

Concrete

12" by 8" by 12" concrete blocks, stuccoed

Anchored to footing as required by code

12"

24'

12"

16" 14'

Plan view

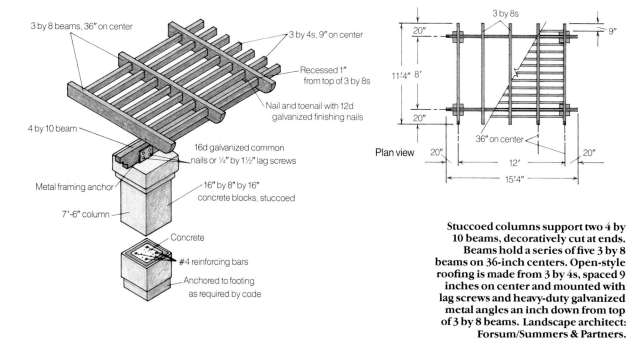

3 by 8 beams, 36" on center

3 by 4s, 9" on center

Recessed 1" from top of 3 by 8s

Nail and toenail with 12d galvanized finishing nails

4 by 10 beam

16d galvanized common nails or ¼" by 1½" lag screws

Metal framing anchor

16" by 8" by 16" concrete blocks, stuccoed

7'-6" column

Concrete

#4 reinforcing bars

Anchored to footing as required by code

3 by 8s

9"

20"

11'4" 8'

20"

Plan view   20"

36" on center

20"

12'

15'4"

Stuccoed columns support two 4 by 10 beams, decoratively cut at ends. Beams hold a series of five 3 by 8 beams on 36-inch centers. Open-style roofing is made from 3 by 4s, spaced 9 inches on center and mounted with lag screws and heavy-duty galvanized metal angles an inch down from top of 3 by 8 beams. Landscape architect: Forsum/Summers & Partners.

■ PARTY PAVILION

Cozy enough for just one or two or with plenty of room for a small crowd, this 12-foot-square gazebolike pavilion offers a deck, benches, and a lath-style roof.

Four posts at each corner rise from the foundation to support the deck, benches, and roof framing. Four ridge beams run from one post at each corner to a 4 by 4 hub, turned on an angle, at the center. The upper edges of these beams are beveled to receive spaced 1 by 2 roofing.

Architect: Thomas Higley.

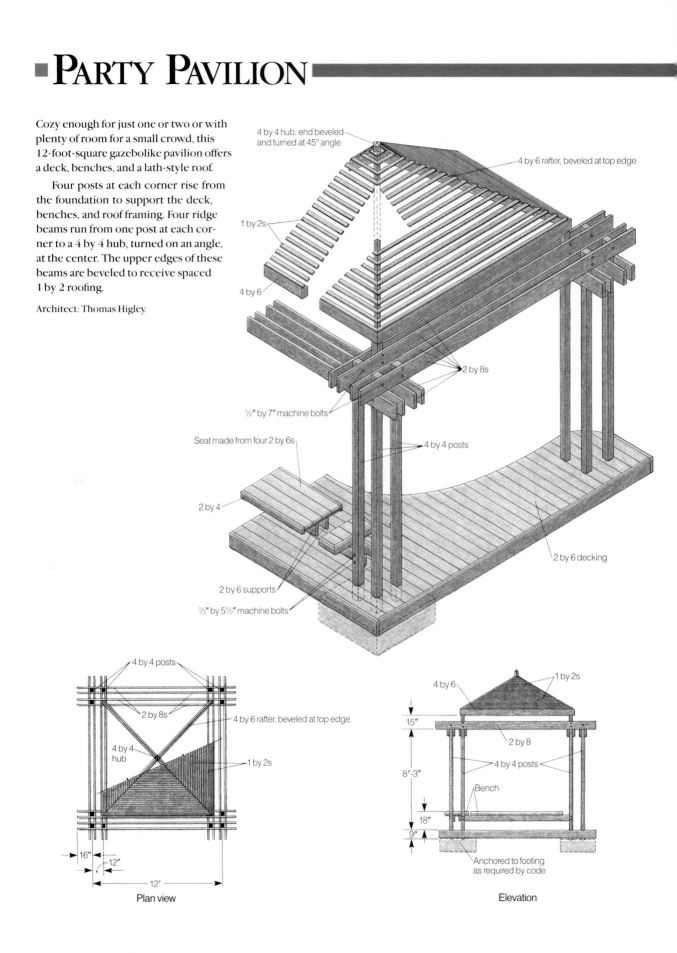

4 by 4 hub, end beveled and turned at 45° angle

4 by 6 rafter, beveled at top edge

1 by 2s

4 by 6

2 by 8s

½" by 7" machine bolts

Seat made from four 2 by 6s

4 by 4 posts

2 by 4

2 by 6 decking

2 by 6 supports

½" by 5½" machine bolts

4 by 4 posts

2 by 8s

4 by 4 hub

4 by 6 rafter, beveled at top edge

1 by 2s

16"   12"

12'

Plan view

4 by 6

1 by 2s

15"

2 by 8

4 by 4 posts

8'-3"

Bench

18"

9"

Anchored to footing as required by code

Elevation

Party-time gazebolike activity center beckons family and friends outdoors.
Quadrupled corner posts tie structure together from foundation to roof.

DINING OCTAGON

Conforming to the contours of an eight-sided brick patio, this handsome pavilion creates a formal outdoor dining space, complete with built-in barbecue. Both the octagonal shape and the careful detailing of posts and beams contribute to the overhead's feeling of formality.

The structure isn't a true octagon; instead, it's slightly elongated. The 6 by 6 posts gain plenty of visual interest from nailed-on, mitered trim, routed with a ½-inch cove bit.

Around the perimeter, 4 by 12 beams, mitered at their ends, rest on the posts. The beams are trimmed with a continuous 2 by 4 fascia. Three 4 by 10 beams run from end to end; matching 4 by 10s, fastened with framing anchors, butt into them and provide blocking between them. All beam ends are cut with a reciprocating or band saw.

Diagonal-patterned prefabricated lattice panels are secured to 2 by 2 nailers.

Because the posts are in contact with the patio, they're made from redwood. The remainder of the structure is built from Douglas fir. All material was resawn at the mill—a special order. Be sure to buy dry lumber and caulk all joints to minimize separation at the miter joints. An opaque stain that blends with the color of the house protects the wood.

Landscape architect: Forsum/Summers & Partners.

Echoing shape of patio, octagonal overhead provides a cool and inviting oasis for al fresco dining and entertaining.

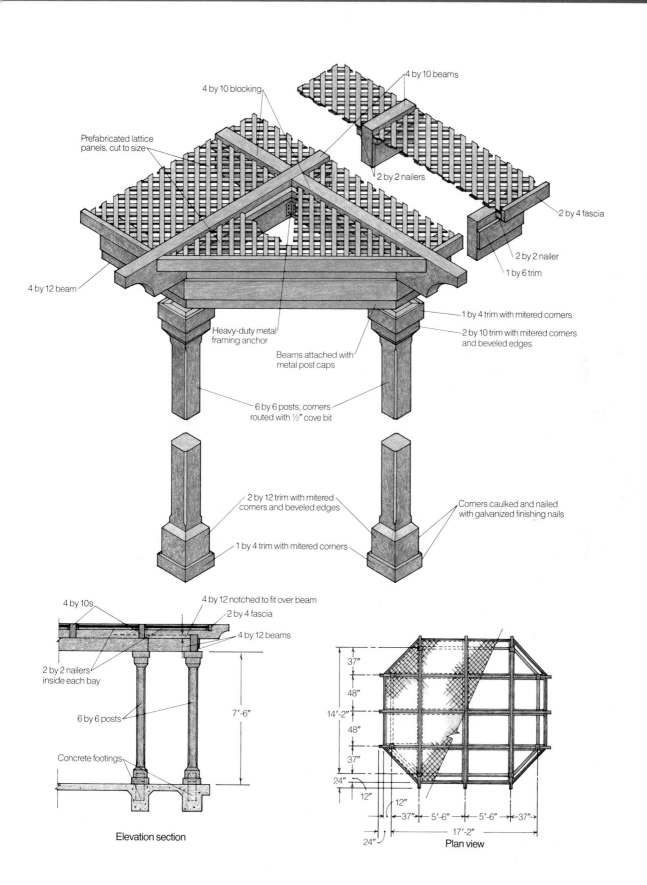

4 by 10 blocking

4 by 10 beams

Prefabricated lattice
panels, cut to size

2 by 2 nailers

2 by 4 fascia

2 by 2 nailer

1 by 6 trim

4 by 12 beam

1 by 4 trim with mitered corners

Heavy-duty metal
framing anchor

2 by 10 trim with mitered corners
and beveled edges

Beams attached with
metal post caps

6 by 6 posts, corners
routed with ½" cove bit

2 by 12 trim with mitered
corners and beveled edges

Corners caulked and nailed
with galvanized finishing nails

1 by 4 trim with mitered corners

4 by 10s

4 by 12 notched to fit over beam

2 by 4 fascia

4 by 12 beams

2 by 2 nailers
inside each bay

6 by 6 posts

7'-6"

Concrete footings

Elevation section

37"

48"

14'-2"

48"

37"

24"

12"

12"

37"

5'-6"

5'-6"

37"

24"

17'-2"

Plan view

REDWOOD CORNER SHELTER

Integrating a freestanding deck with a shade-casting overhead, this informal entertainment area nestles into a corner of a small backyard. With built-in benches, bamboo shades for privacy, potted plants, and seating, it creates a comfortable stage for outdoor entertaining.

The entire structure, from decking to roofing, is built from redwood. Posts made from 6 by 6s support the deck, benches, and roof. The roof of spaced 3 by 3s (a special-order size) rests on 2 by 10 beams that bolt to each side of the posts.

Landscape architect: Rudy Yadao Associates.

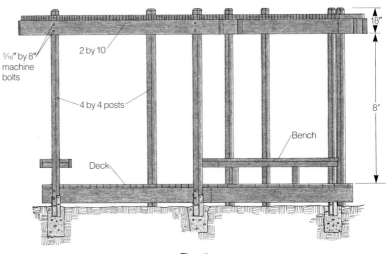

5/16" by 8" machine bolts

2 by 10

4 by 4 posts

Bench

Deck

18"

8'

Elevation

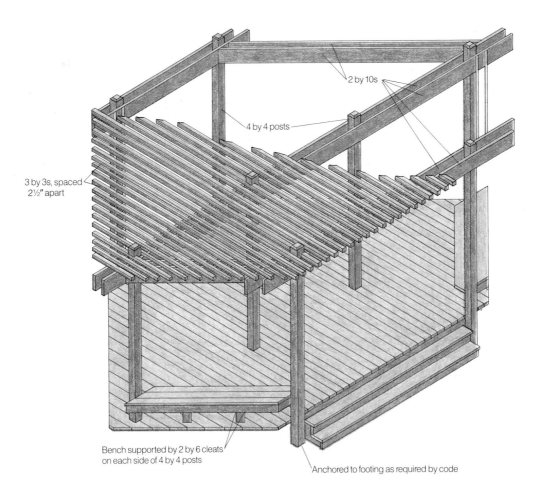

2 by 10s

4 by 4 posts

3 by 3s, spaced 2½" apart

Bench supported by 2 by 6 cleats on each side of 4 by 4 posts

Anchored to footing as required by code

Redwood 3 by 3s and bamboo blinds work together to screen harsh afternoon sunlight, setting the stage for comfortable garden entertaining.

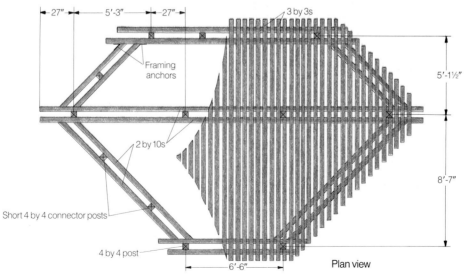

27" 5'-3" 27"

3 by 3s

Framing anchors

5'-1½"

2 by 10s

8'-7"

Short 4 by 4 connector posts

4 by 4 post

6'-6"

Plan view

■ STATELY CORNER TRELLIS

Defining a backyard corner and framing a panoramic view, this distinctive open-style overhead makes room for a picturesque Brazilian pepper tree, which, in turn, contributes its shade to the patio area below.

Posts are 6 by 6s with 1 by 4s nailed to each face. At post tops, a capital is created from 1 by 2s and 2 by 3s, mitered at the corners. Heavy-duty metal post anchors lock the posts to the concrete slab and footings.

The "roof" is made entirely from 4 by 8 and 4 by 10 beams. To cut the decorative pattern at the beam ends, mark and cut one short beam, using a reciprocating saw or band saw, and then use it as a pattern for marking the others. The 4 by 8s are notched to lock on top of the 4 by 10s. (Mark all matching pieces at the same time to simplify the work.)

This structure is made from surfaced Douglas fir, primed and painted with two coats of semigloss enamel after assembly. Be sure to caulk and fill all joints, cracks, and holes before applying the final coat of paint.

Landscape architect: Forsum/Summers & Partners.

Framing a Brazilian pepper tree, this simple corner trellis shelters and defines outer limits of patio.

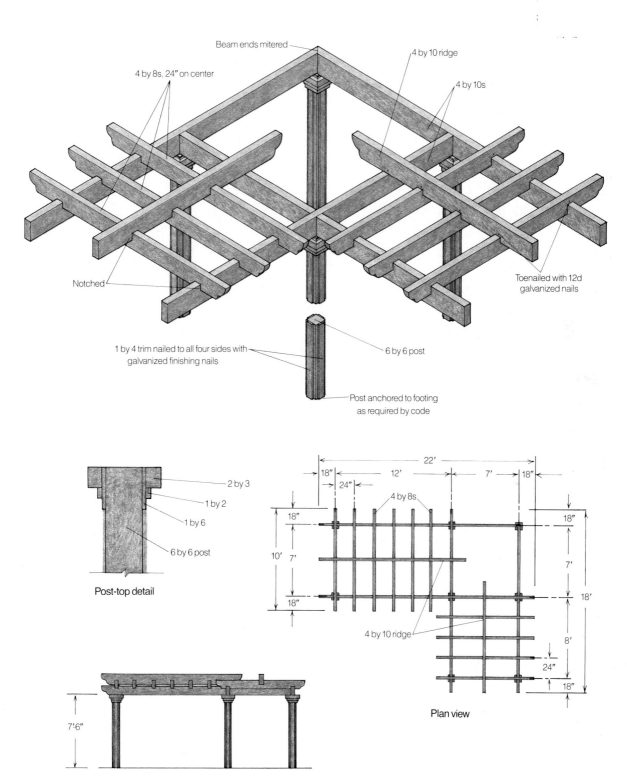

Beam ends mitered

4 by 8s, 24" on center

4 by 10 ridge

4 by 10s

Notched

Toenailed with 12d galvanized nails

1 by 4 trim nailed to all four sides with galvanized finishing nails

6 by 6 post

Post anchored to footing as required by code

2 by 3

1 by 2

1 by 6

6 by 6 post

Post-top detail

22'

18'

12'

7'

18'

24'

18'

18'

10'

7'

18'

4 by 8s

4 by 10 ridge

18'

7'

18'

8'

24'

18'

Plan view

7'6"

Elevation

HOUSE-ATTACHED PAVILION

The elegance of this structure comes partially from its posts and beams—they're clad with built-up trim, some of it beveled and mitered—and partially from its overall design: the beams and upper-level roof make it quite an eye-catcher.

Unlike most house-attached patio roofs, this shelter is linked to the house only by a pair of beams. The overhead's shape mimics the patio below.

Beneath the light-toned stain is resawn Douglas fir (the posts are redwood). All joints are carefully caulked to keep moisture out.

Landscape architect: Forsum/Summers & Partners.

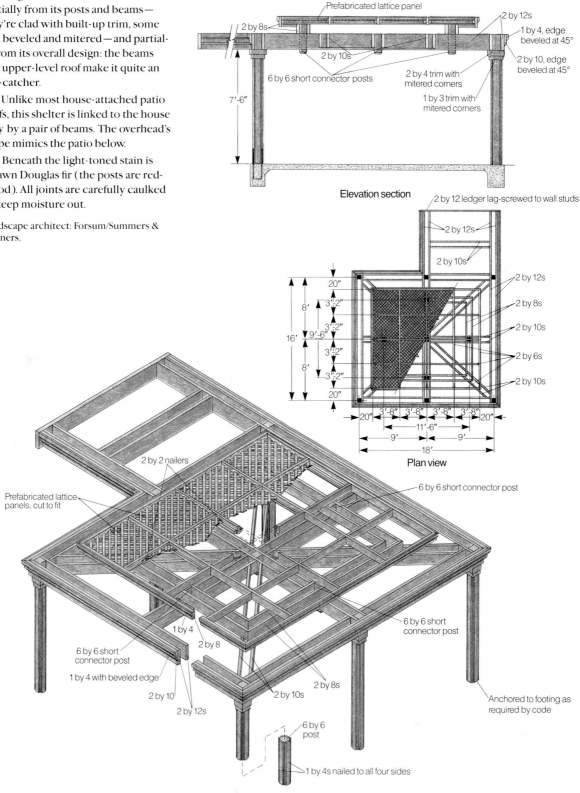

Elevation section

Plan view

Beams converge at center of this expansive poolside retreat. Paired beams, extending from one side, are overhead's only link to house. Photo at right shows corner post detail.

■COVERED CABAÑA

Simple rectangular lines allow this structure to blend in with almost any contemporary setting. The cabaña offers a solid, built-up roof for shedding rain and shading guests. Posts made from 4 by 4s and lattice panels articulate the design and complement the brick patio.

To support the roof, 2 by 10s run around the perimeter. Rafters made from 2 by 6s and mounted on joist hangers are spaced on 20-inch centers. Additional 2 by 6 blocking runs along the center points of the rafters. Both rafters and blocking hold ⅝-inch rough-sawn plywood siding (good face down) that provides the base for the roofing material. (The plywood's edges are centered over rafters or blocking.)

The redwood posts are attached to the patio with metal post anchors. Prefabricated lattice panels are sandwiched between 1 by 2s attached to the posts.

Landscape architect: Bill Hays.

Blocking sun and rain alike, roomy cabaña with simple, uncomplicated lines offers all-weather cover.

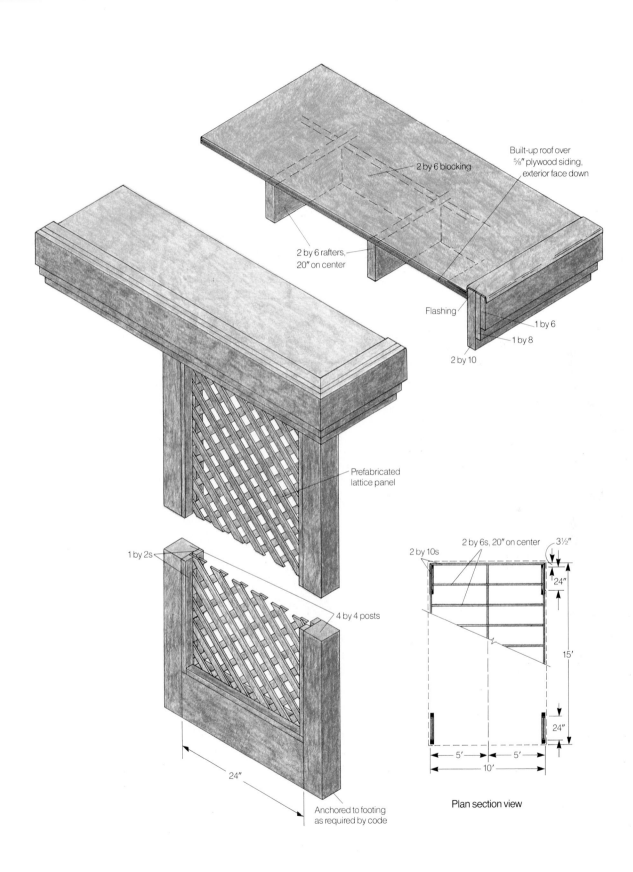

Built-up roof over ⅝″ plywood siding, exterior face down

2 by 6 blocking

2 by 6 rafters, 20″ on center

Flashing

1 by 6

1 by 8

2 by 10

Prefabricated lattice panel

1 by 2s

4 by 4 posts

24″

Anchored to footing as required by code

2 by 10s

2 by 6s, 20″ on center

3½″

24″

15′

24″

5′

5′

10′

Plan section view

■SPACE FRAMES

Like the "Emperor's new clothes"—more implied than real—the structures shown here prove the premise that it doesn't take much to define an outdoor area. Little more than posts connected at the tops by pairs of 2 by 6s, these open space frames create a sense of enclosure, whether over an expansive patio (at right) or a small deck (below).

Landscape architect: Michael Whitmore and Associates for the American Wood Council.

Large space frame, turned at a 45° angle to front of house for visual interest, defines space, yet still allows light to penetrate inside house.

Rising from a riverbank, four 6 by 6 pressure-treated posts support a 12-foot-square deck and its simple "no-roof" roof. Posts extend 12 inches above pairs of 2 by 6s that define perimeter. For visual interest, post tops are beveled and notched. Railing of 4 by 4s, 2 by 6s, and 2 by 2s encloses space.

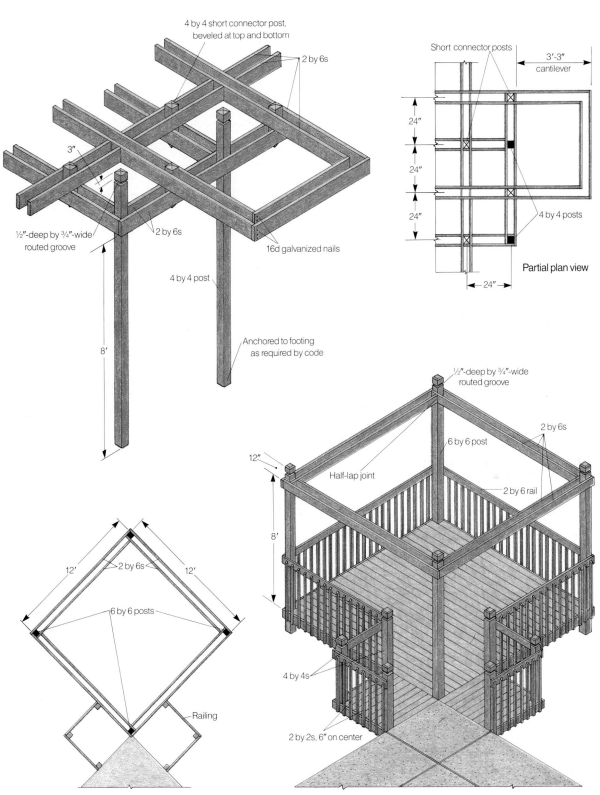

4 by 4 short connector post, beveled at top and bottom

2 by 6s

3″

½″-deep by ¾″-wide routed groove

2 by 6s

16d galvanized nails

4 by 4 post

Anchored to footing as required by code

8′

Short connector posts

3′-3″ cantilever

24″

24″

24″

4 by 4 posts

24″

Partial plan view

½″-deep by ¾″-wide routed groove

6 by 6 post

2 by 6s

Half-lap joint

2 by 6 rail

12″

8′

4 by 4s

2 by 2s, 6″ on center

12′

2 by 6s

12′

6 by 6 posts

Railing

Plan view

■ SHADE ARCADES

Casting partial shade on their respec-
tive houses and defining pathways and
patio areas, the overheads pictured on
these two pages illustrate how a patio
roof can integrate a house with such
landscape elements as walkways, patio,
lawn, pool, and planting beds. Both
structures feature arcades that nestle
up against the walls of the house, even
as they reach out to encompass the
garden.

Landscape architect: Rogers Gardens.

**Widely spaced beams extend over spa
and end of pool. Narrow, freestanding
arcade shades house from afternoon
sun. Structure is made from rough-
sawn fir, stained to complement
house trim.**

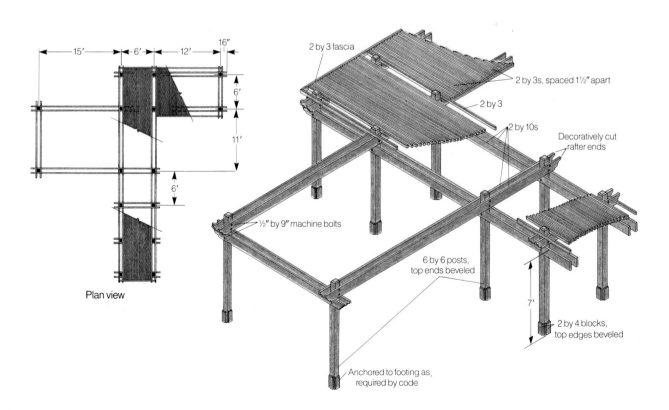

Plan view

2 by 3 fascia

2 by 3s, spaced 1½" apart

2 by 3

2 by 10s

Decoratively cut
rafter ends

½" by 9" machine bolts

6 by 6 posts,
top ends beveled

7'

2 by 4 blocks,
top edges beveled

Anchored to footing as
required by code

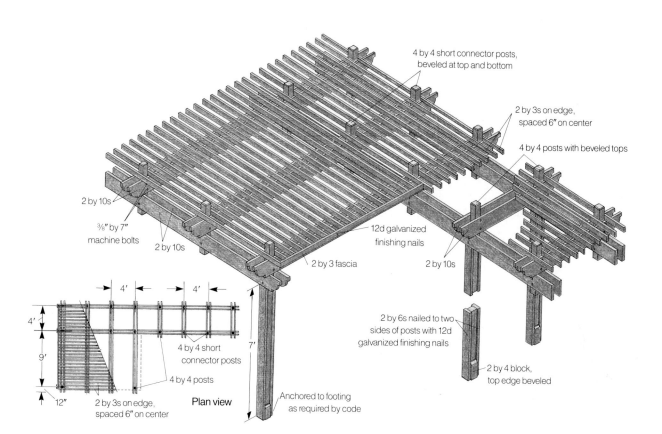

4 by 4 short connector posts,
beveled at top and bottom

2 by 3s on edge,
spaced 6" on center

4 by 4 posts with beveled tops

2 by 10s

⅜" by 7"
machine bolts

2 by 10s

12d galvanized
finishing nails

2 by 3 fascia

2 by 10s

2 by 6s nailed to two
sides of posts with 12d
galvanized finishing nails

2 by 4 block,
top edge beveled

Anchored to footing
as required by code

4'   4'

4'

9'

12"

4 by 4 short
connector posts

4 by 4 posts

2 by 3s on edge,
spaced 6" on center

7'

Plan view

**Narrow walkway overhead widens to
include entertainment patio. Short
connector posts join perpendicular
beams, yet don't interfere with sight
lines. Open-style roofing is made
from 2 by 3s turned on edge and
spaced on 6-inch centers. Surfaced
lumber is painted.**

CLASSIC REVIVAL

A cross between Post-modern architecture and a Greco-Roman temple, this pavilion offers a dramatic setting for poolside repose. Bold, round columns support a classically styled, cross-hatched roof.

Beneath the stuccoed exterior of each post is a pressure-treated 4 by 4, anchored to the concrete patio and footing with a sturdy metal post anchor. Like the spokes of a wheel, 2 by 4s radiate from that center post to form a framework for the stucco. The 2 by 12 beams are bolted to the posts; intermediate 2 by 10s are bolted to the inner beams for additional support.

Above, a layer of 2 by 2s on 12-inch centers is crisscrossed by a second layer. The top is wrapped with 2 by 4s, mitered at the corners.

The structure, made primarily from Douglas fir, is primed and painted with two coats of semigloss enamel.

Landscape architect: Forsum/Summers & Partners.

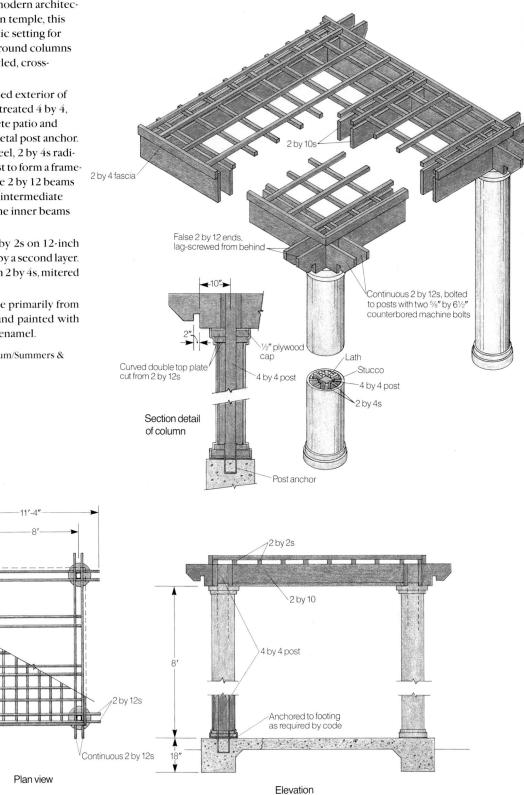

2 by 10s

2 by 4 fascia

False 2 by 12 ends, lag-screwed from behind

Continuous 2 by 12s, bolted to posts with two ⅝" by 6½" counterbored machine bolts

←10"→

2"

½" plywood cap

Curved double top plate cut from 2 by 12s

4 by 4 post

Lath

Stucco

4 by 4 post

2 by 4s

Section detail of column

Post anchor

11'-4"

20"   8'

20"

4'

15'-4"

4'

4'

2 by 12s

Continuous 2 by 12s

Plan view

2 by 2s

2 by 10

4 by 4 post

8'

Anchored to footing as required by code

18"

Elevation

A retreat for sun worshippers,
dramatic poolside monument offers
partial relief from sun's searing afternoon rays.

OUTDOOR FABRICS

Colorful, lightweight, capable of deflecting rain and diffusing sun—these are just a few of the attributes of canvas-style roofing. The following section discusses several different ways of making and installing a fabric roof and offers suggestions on caring for the roof once it's up. (For information on the different kinds of fabrics you can use for roofing, see page 13.)

Design & Installation

A fabric roof is typically made from both fabric and a framework that supports it and gives it shape. The framework may be made from pipes, rods, tubing, wood—whatever material works. Pipes and rods are frequently used because they offer maximum support with minimum visibility.

The canvas top can be strapped or laced to the frame, or casings that slide over the framework can be sewn in the fabric.

Often, awning makers can make the entire roof. They design the fabric's pattern and the framework that will support it, sew the pieces together, decide on the method of attachment, and have a frame welded to the correct specifications.

Making the canvas roof. Most outdoor fabrics come in widths of 46 inches, though 60-inch widths are sometimes available. Unless your design utilizes just single widths, it's likely that pieces will have to be sewn together. If you have the right sewing equipment and skills, you can do the sewing yourself.

Though you can sew 10-ounce duck on most sewing machines, fabric that's vinyl-coated or painted is best entrusted to an awning shop. Canvas heavier than 10-ounce weight must be sewn with special equipment. (It is possible to hand-sew canvas, using a No. 13 sailmaker's needle, but—as you might guess—this can be excessively tedious work if the cover is large.)

If you do sew your own cover, be sure to buy the thread from the canvas dealer.

Lacing fabric on a framework. A typical method of fastening an outdoor fabric to a frame is to lace it on by threading nylon rope or cord through grommets that have been installed around the fabric's perimeter. An awning shop will put the grommets in for you at a minimal charge, or you can buy a simple kit and do it yourself. Either way, make sure grommets fall at each corner and every 8 inches along the edges.

If you don't like the look of laced-on canvas, cut the canvas extra long so you can lap the edges around the frame and lace them together across the top, out of view.

Using casings. Another method of attachment is to sew casings, or sleeves, along the edges of the fabric and then slip frame members through them. This method requires very accurate measurements, and installation can be difficult. Also, tension across the fabric can be irregular, wrinkling and bunching can occur, and, over time, the fabric can sag.

Be aware that fabric mounted this way may not be easily adjustable if it begins to sag, nor can it be removed easily for repair, maintenance, or storage.

Making an adjustable system. You can make an adjustable overhead by suspending fabric from strong cables (see above, at right). With this system, the fabric can be shifted over the patio—extended to cover a certain area or perhaps retracted to open up another.

This type of cover is usually made up of a series of 5-foot-wide strips that run parallel to each other. Wider pieces can be used, but they may be cumbersome to move back and forth on the cables; they're also liable to sail off in a strong wind.

To make an adjustable cover, attach

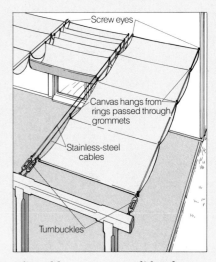

Adjustable canvas cover slides along taut cables.

a stainless-steel cable to the house or frame with large screw eyes or awning hinges. Add a turnbuckle at one end of the cable to take up slack. Suspend the fabric from rings passed through grommets along the fabric's edges.

Maintenance

A modest maintenance program will allow outdoor fabrics to last as long as possible. Keeping them clean does the most good. Don't let dirt, leaves, or other debris accumulate on top—they can cause stains or promote the growth of mildew. (On synthetics, mildew grows on the debris, not on the fabric.)

Sweep the fabric occasionally with a clean household broom and hose it down from time to time. When you need to do a more thorough cleaning, use a mild, natural soap (not a detergent) and thoroughly rinse off all traces.

Be very careful when using insecticides and other sprays near an outdoor fabric; they can cause permanent stains and reduce the fabric's water repellency. And never barbecue under a fabric shade—there's always a danger of fire and smoke damage.

Pleated pentagon of blue acrylic fabric laced to a welded steel frame covers poolside ramada. Stuccoed columns support 25-foot-wide structure. Landscape architects: Guy Greene and Stephen Acuña.

ENTRY SHADE-MAKER

Lattice panels run the length of this house (shown on facing page), forming a shaded gallery for walking and sitting. Because the house provides structural stability for the overhead, construction is simple, despite the project's large scale.

The 4 by 4 posts, anchored to concrete footings, are made from redwood. Outside posts have 2 by 3s nailed to each face; interior posts have 1 by 12 trim, mitered at the corners, nailed to their bases.

Heavy-duty framing anchors connect beams where they intersect. The prefabricated lattice panels, cut to fit, are placed on 2 by 2s nailed along the beams.

Landscape architect: The Peridian Group.

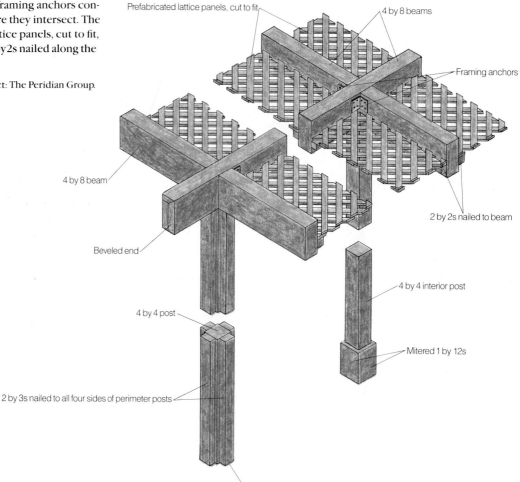

Prefabricated lattice panels, cut to fit

4 by 8 beams

Framing anchors

4 by 8 beam

2 by 2s nailed to beam

Beveled end

4 by 4 interior post

4 by 4 post

Mitered 1 by 12s

2 by 3s nailed to all four sides of perimeter posts

Anchored to footing as required by code

Lattice overhead, extending from house's eave lines, shades house and offers informal cover at entrance.

CONTEMPORARY ELEGANCE

Attached to the house at only one corner, this patio roof is a careful extension of the home's architecture. The overhead's boxy lines and detailing complement the home's contemporary styling.

The structure is an egg-crate formation of 4 by 8 and 4 by 10 beams, mounted on 6 by 6 redwood posts. Its charm results from its built-up trim: both 1-by and 2-by stock has been mitered, beveled, and nailed to posts and beams. False partial posts—like movie-set facades— attach to the house walls to complete the theme. Roofing of 3 by 3s, spaced on 10-inch centers, allows more sun than shade.

All seams and joints are caulked to minimize warping and moisture damage. The wood, surfaced Douglas fir except for the posts, is painted to blend with the house trim.

Architect: Forsum/Summers & Partners.

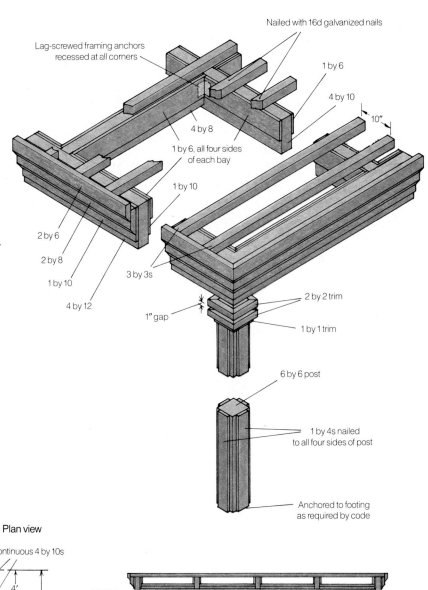

Nailed with 16d galvanized nails

Lag-screwed framing anchors recessed at all corners

1 by 6

4 by 10

10"

4 by 8

1 by 6, all four sides of each bay

1 by 10

2 by 6

2 by 8

1 by 10

3 by 3s

4 by 12

1" gap

2 by 2 trim

1 by 1 trim

6 by 6 post

1 by 4s nailed to all four sides of post

Anchored to footing as required by code

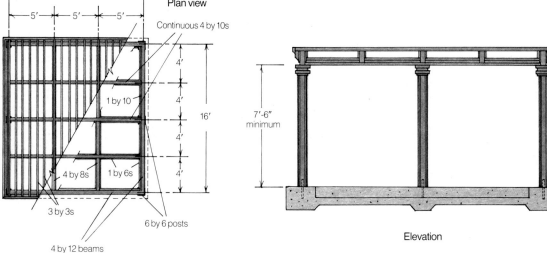

15'

5'   5'   5'

Plan view

Continuous 4 by 10s

4'

1 by 10

4'

16'

4'

4'

4 by 8s   1 by 6s

3 by 3s

6 by 6 posts

4 by 12 beams

7'-6" minimum

Elevation

Only one corner of this dignified patio roof ties to house. At connection point, trim has been carefully detailed to mimic posts. Mitered trim, built-up on beams and posts (see detail photos), creates stylish elegance.

▪ GARDEN RETREATS

Nestled in lush surroundings, the retreats shown here and on the facing page are shady places for reading, relaxation, and quiet contemplation—escapes from the frantic pace of everyday life.

Resting on an exposed aggregate slab, this retreat is built from sturdy "construction heart" redwood, brushed with bleaching oil for an immediate driftwood-gray effect. A bell-shaped lamp provides evening illumination. Architect: Hooper, Olmsted & Hrovat for the California Redwood Association. Landscape architect: Casey A. Kawamoto.

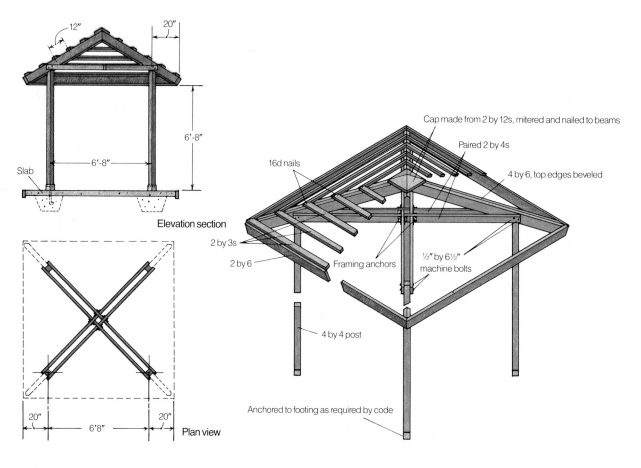

12″
20″

6′-8″

Slab

6′-8″

Elevation section

20″   20″
6′8″
Plan view

Cap made from 2 by 12s, mitered and nailed to beams

Paired 2 by 4s

16d nails

4 by 6, top edges beveled

2 by 3s

2 by 6

Framing anchors

½″ by 6½″ machine bolts

4 by 4 post

Anchored to footing as required by code

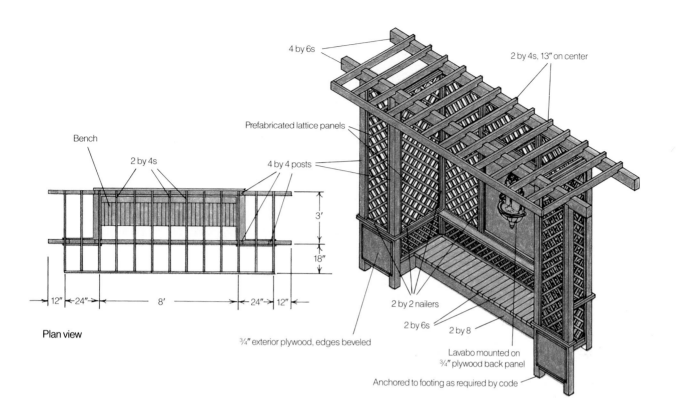

4 by 6s

2 by 4s, 13" on center

Prefabricated lattice panels

Bench

2 by 4s

4 by 4 posts

3'

18"

12" — 24" — 8' — 24" — 12"

Plan view

¾" exterior plywood, edges beveled

2 by 2 nailers

2 by 6s

2 by 8

Lavabo mounted on ¾" plywood back panel

Anchored to footing as required by code

Vining plants climb over charming garden bench, made from prefabricated lattice panels mounted on 4 by 4 posts. Rafters are 2 by 4s spaced on 13-inch centers. Lavabo accents panel on bench back. Landscape architect: Bill Derringer.

▪Entryways That Welcome

Arbors can create magic at a home's entry, as shown on these two pages. Often combined with a fence and gate, an entry arbor is a mood setter, a dramatic way of welcoming guests. Of course, arbors can be functional, too. They can create shade or shelter, as well as provide structural support for gate posts.

Elegant articulation of elements marks this strongly linear, yet friendly, garden entry (photo shows its inner side). L-shaped deck and shade shelter give an almost ceremonial sense of entrance, while openwork gate and flanking "wing-wall" fences offer glimpses of lush, serene garden within. Landscape architect: Kawasaki/Theilacker & Associates.

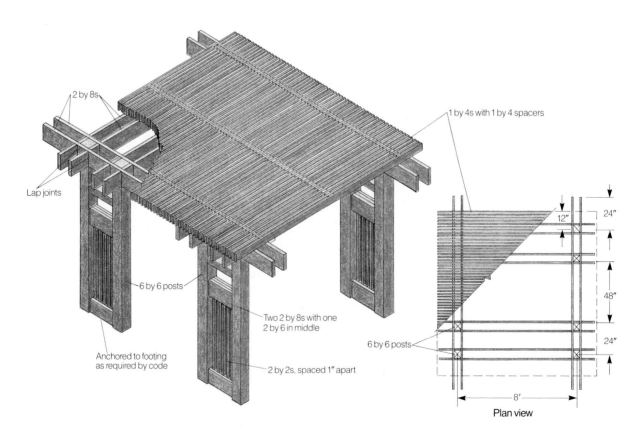

2 by 8s

Lap joints

1 by 4s with 1 by 4 spacers

6 by 6 posts

Two 2 by 8s with one 2 by 6 in middle

Anchored to footing as required by code

2 by 2s, spaced 1" apart

6 by 6 posts

12"

24"

48"

24"

8'

Plan view

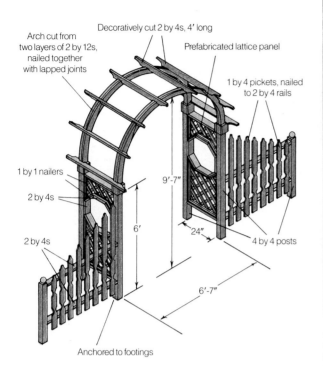

Arch cut from two layers of 2 by 12s, nailed together with lapped joints

Decoratively cut 2 by 4s, 4' long

Prefabricated lattice panel

1 by 4 pickets, nailed to 2 by 4 rails

1 by 1 nailers

2 by 4s

2 by 4s

9'-7"

6'

24"

4 by 4 posts

6'-7"

Anchored to footings

Arching entry trellis invites guests to front door. Arch is built from a double thickness of 2 by 12s cut into arcs and nailed together; joints are staggered between front and back sections. Resulting arch is sanded, caulked, and painted to hide joints. For sides, prefabricated lattice panels are cut to fit framing. Design: Philip Neumann.

Bold stucco columns support scant roofing of open beams. This entry blends perfectly with house and wall; for a view of matching patio roof in backyard, see page 25. Landscape architect: Forsum/Summers & Partners.

■Hardworking Garden Trellises

Trellises can be both hardworking and decorative. Functionally, they support vining plants. In vegetable gardens, such as the one shown on the facing page, a trellis can be a necessity for growing beans or vining grapes. Decoratively, a trellis can add height and design interest to the garden or yard.

Building a trellis is normally a simple job. Most are supported by a single line of posts, and, as both of these trellises show, you can tie the construction to a fence or planter box.

Garden work center hides behind an attractive, trellis-topped fence. Trellis design can be adapted easily to work without a fence. Landscape architect: Bill Derringer.

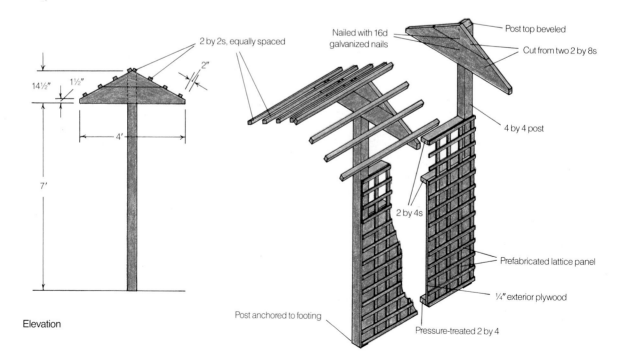

2 by 2s, equally spaced

2″

14½″   1½″

4′

7′

Elevation

Nailed with 16d galvanized nails

Post top beveled

Cut from two 2 by 8s

4 by 4 post

2 by 4s

Prefabricated lattice panel

¼″ exterior plywood

Post anchored to footing

Pressure-treated 2 by 4

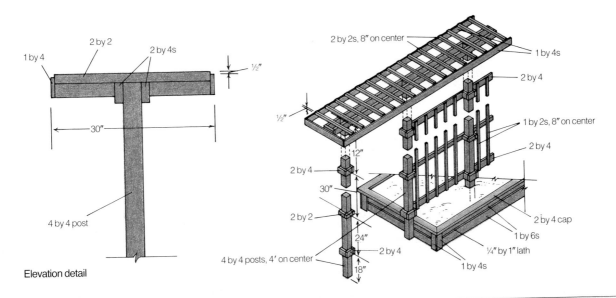

2 by 2
1 by 4
2 by 4s
½"
30"
4 by 4 post

Elevation detail

2 by 2s, 8" on center
1 by 4s
2 by 4
½"
1 by 2s, 8" on center
2 by 4
12"
2 by 4
30"
2 by 2
2 by 4 cap
24"
2 by 4
1 by 6s
¼" by 1" lath
4 by 4 posts, 4' on center
1 by 4s
18"

Draped with beans and grape vines, garden-defining trellis rises from raised bed. For a bit of whimsy, trim pieces are mitered and nailed onto 4 by 4 posts. Landscape architect: John Herbst.

GAZEBOS

When you think of a gazebo, do you imagine an elaborately detailed summerhouse for entertaining guests or a simple garden retreat where you can relax and watch the setting sun? Perhaps you picture a classic latticework Victorian gazebo. Or you may envision a more contemporary, sophisticated design.

Many different kinds of structures are called gazebos. On the following pages, you'll discover gazebo designs representative of that variety, as well as information on gazebo kits.

Traditional latticework gazebo, set amid towering trees, reflects charm of an earlier era.

■ ROMANTIC GAZEBO

The gazebo shown on the facing page, with its lacy latticework arches and railings, offers a place of irresistible charm for quiet enjoyment of the garden. This, like nearly any gazebo, can be built on either a patio slab or a deck. Here's how it's done.

Build four complete wall panels and four sets of framed lath panels (less one bottom panel for the doorway) for linking the sections. Working on a flat surface, use one piece as a pattern for matching pieces. Use the frames as patterns for marking the cuts on the prefabricated lattice panels.

Prime and paint the lattice, posts, frames, and rafters before assembly (you'll need to touch them up later). With several helpers, stand the completed sections up and join them together with the framed lath panels, leaving the bolts at the top loose for easier assembly of the rafters later on. Bolt the wall panels to the deck or patio surface, too.

Lap and screw long and short rafter pieces together. After drilling pilot and countersink holes, lag-screw each assembled rafter to the octagonal center hub. Again with several helpers, lift

the assembled rafters into place, aligning rafter ends with the tops of the posts. Make sure the rafters are tight against the spacers. Drill pilot holes and lag-screw the rafters to the posts. Tighten all bolts.

Roof with lap siding. Caulk along the hips and roof them with shingles.

Design: Gazebo Nostalgia.

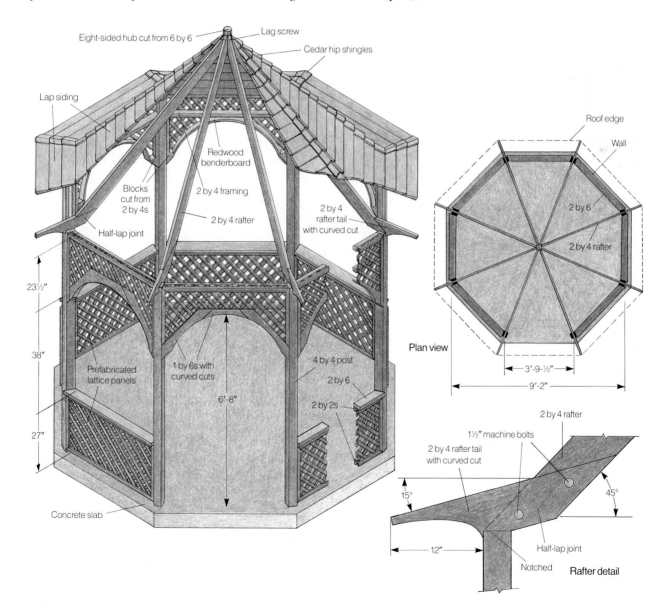

Eight-sided hub cut from 6 by 6 — Lag screw
Cedar hip shingles
Lap siding
Redwood benderboard
Blocks cut from 2 by 4s
2 by 4 framing
2 by 4 rafter
Half-lap joint
2 by 4 rafter tail with curved cut
23½"
Prefabricated lattice panels
1 by 6s with curved cuts
38"
4 by 4 post
2 by 6
6'-8"
27"
2 by 2s
Concrete slab

Roof edge
Wall
2 by 6
2 by 4 rafter
Plan view
3'-9-½"
9'-2"

2 by 4 rafter
1½" machine bolts
2 by 4 rafter tail with curved cut
15°
45°
Half-lap joint
12"
Notched
Rafter detail

CEDAR CATHEDRAL

A grove of lanky cedar trees provides a dignified setting for a gazebo tailored to adult entertaining. Groups of cedar posts support built-in benches and the open-rafter roof.

Between the posts at the ends of the benches are built-in planters that add seasonal color. A series of 1 by 2s wrap the post tops, creating texture and visual interest. The 2 by 6 rafters overlap at the ridge; 1 by 4s nailed to each side of the rafters enhance the detailing.

Trim is fitted to the bottom of the posts at deck level; the posts, however, continue down beneath the gazebo's decking, where they're supported by footings.

The cedar's natural finish will keep it looking good for years.

Architect: Robert C. Slenes and Morton Safford James III for Bennett, Johnson, Slenes & Smith.

Airy gazebo's sophisticated design, uncluttered lines, and natural finish perfectly complement its serene setting.

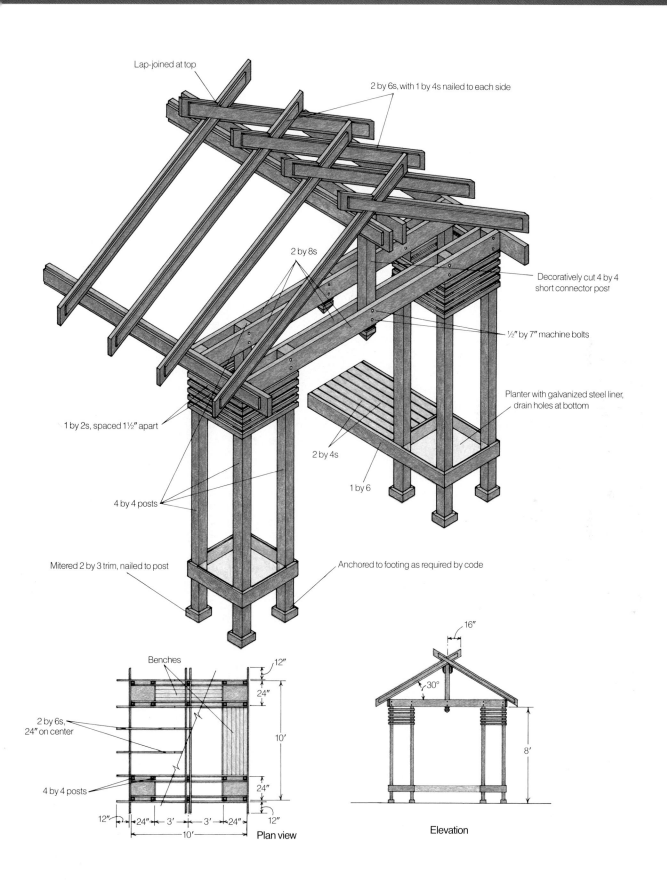

Lap-joined at top

2 by 6s, with 1 by 4s nailed to each side

2 by 8s

Decoratively cut 4 by 4 short connector post

½″ by 7″ machine bolts

1 by 2s, spaced 1½″ apart

Planter with galvanized steel liner, drain holes at bottom

2 by 4s

1 by 6

4 by 4 posts

Mitered 2 by 3 trim, nailed to post

Anchored to footing as required by code

Benches

12″

24″

2 by 6s, 24″ on center

10′

4 by 4 posts

24″

12″

24″

3′

3′

24″

12″

10′

Plan view

16″

30°

8′

Elevation

INSTANT GAZEBOS: FROM KITS

If building your own gazebo from scratch sounds a bit overwhelming, you may want to consider a gazebo kit. Several companies manufacture gazebos that you can purchase in kit form, complete except for the foundation. You construct the gazebo on a slab, deck, or foundation of piers or crushed stone. For some types, assembly — with a helper — takes a weekend or two and requires only basic tools and skills.

Depending on size, material, and style, kits are available from as little as $500 to as much as $20,000; most are in the $2,000 to $4,000 range. These prices are often less than the cost of having a custom gazebo designed and built by a professional builder, even if you buy the kit and pay a carpenter to do the assembly.

Buying a gazebo kit can be a major investment, so before you buy, be sure you know what you're getting. Cheap materials and poor workmanship are no bargain at any price. A poorly made gazebo may not survive a harsh winter. Connections should be made with galvanized or brass hardware, and machining should be carefully done so assembly is relatively easy. Details, such as railings or bracing, are worthy of close scrutiny. Also, be sure to read the assembly directions beforehand to see if they're easy to follow.

Find out whether the gazebo is made from redwood or cedar heartwoods or from less-expensive pressure-treated lumber. Can the wood be finished naturally or must it be painted?

Also, make sure you know what's included in the price of the kit. Who pays for delivery? This is important, because a gazebo may weigh 1,500 pounds or more. Is flooring and floor framing included? What about benches, screens, and steps? Many kits allow you to choose between open railings or lattice panels and other similar details.

If you're not able to see an actual example of the gazebo, ask the company for names of customers. They can tell you whether they were satisfied with the company's service and the quality of the workmanship.

Here are a few tips to keep in mind if you use a gazebo kit:
• Plan the site carefully; remember that most kit gazebos are permanent once they're assembled.
• Be sure to anchor the gazebo properly; otherwise a heavy wind might blow it over.
• If you put the gazebo on a concrete slab, make sure that you pitch the slab for rain runoff.
• Follow the manufacturer's instructions closely, paying special attention to the building sequence and to techniques for anchoring the gazebo, fastening joints, and finishing.

Upward sweeping roofline caps poolside gazebo. This kit gazebo, measuring more than 10 feet across, arrives primed on exterior surfaces. From Bow House, Inc., Bolton, MA.

Generous 15-foot gazebo offers plenty of space for outdoor activities and makes a grand statement in garden. Built from western red cedar, it takes a natural finish beautifully. Kit's basic elements, which go together easily with hand tools, are shown above. From Vixen Hill Manufacturing Co., Elverson, PA.

Like a small-town bandstand of the early 1900s, this gazebo has open grillwork sides and a fabric canopy. It measures 13 feet from wall to wall. Framework is made from aluminum castings and extrusions, prewelded for quick on-site assembly. From Moultrie Manufacturing Co., Moultrie, GA.

GARDEN GAZEBO

A light and airy octagonal pavilion, this garden gazebo provides space for informal outdoor meals and a perch for a comfortable porch swing. Lap siding on the roof sheds rain and shades the interior. The gazebo measures 12 feet across; the deck it sits on extends an additional 2 feet. A 36-inch-diameter cupola accents the top.

Though this gazebo sits on a deck, it could just as easily be built on a patio slab. It's designed so the wall sections can be prefabricated on the ground, then raised and bolted to each other and to the deck or patio. The decorative railing slats are 1 by 6s.

The latticework along the top is made from manufactured lattice panels; the framing serves as a pattern for marking the cuts. (Building any gazebo involves a lot of replication—there are

generally at least eight of nearly every part. It's usually possible to use one piece as a pattern for marking, cutting, or drilling like pieces.)

For rafters, 2 by 4s extend from posts to a hexagonal hub. The rafters are joined to the hub on the ground; then the assembly is lifted into place, with the rafter ends between the 2 by 4 uprights, and the rafters are bolted to the uprights. The cupola is framed separately and screwed to rafter tops. For roofing, lap siding is nailed to rafters and other framing supports.

All joints are caulked and the structure is primed with an oil- or alkyd-base undercoat. Finally, exterior latex enamel is brushed on. The roofing is finished with two coats of clear water repellent.

Design: Gazebo Nostalgia.

Lap siding, securely fastened to framing members, provides a solid covering for gazebo.

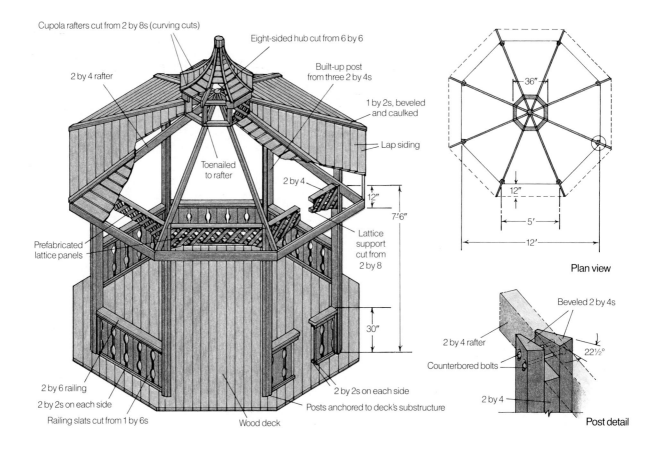

Cupola rafters cut from 2 by 8s (curving cuts)

Eight-sided hub cut from 6 by 6

2 by 4 rafter

Built-up post from three 2 by 4s

1 by 2s, beveled and caulked

Lap siding

Toenailed to rafter

2 by 4

12"

7'6"

Lattice support cut from 2 by 8

Prefabricated lattice panels

2 by 6 railing

2 by 2s on each side

Railing slats cut from 1 by 6s

Wood deck

Posts anchored to deck's substructure

2 by 2s on each side

30"

36"

12"

5'

12'

Plan view

Beveled 2 by 4s

2 by 4 rafter

Counterbored bolts

22½°

2 by 4

Post detail

Traditional in feeling and design, cheerful gazebo in midst of garden offers a place for open-air dining and relaxation.

FANTASY GAZEBO

Viewed from the front, the billowy, exotically layered roof of this backyard temple looks solid. Actually, it's made from equally spaced 2 by 12s set on edge. They rest on the top plate of a shallow structure, reinforced by a built-in bench along the back.

A compressed hexagon 8 feet deep and 10 feet long comprises the base shape. Made from 17 pairs of 2 by 12s spaced 6 inches apart, the roof rises to 14 feet at its peak. The curvilinear pattern cut in the top of each board follows the same rhythm, but as each pair gets progressively wider and higher, the shape of each peak changes. Copper straps mask each center joint. Threaded rods running through copper pipes space the roof layers.

Architect: Mark Hajjar.

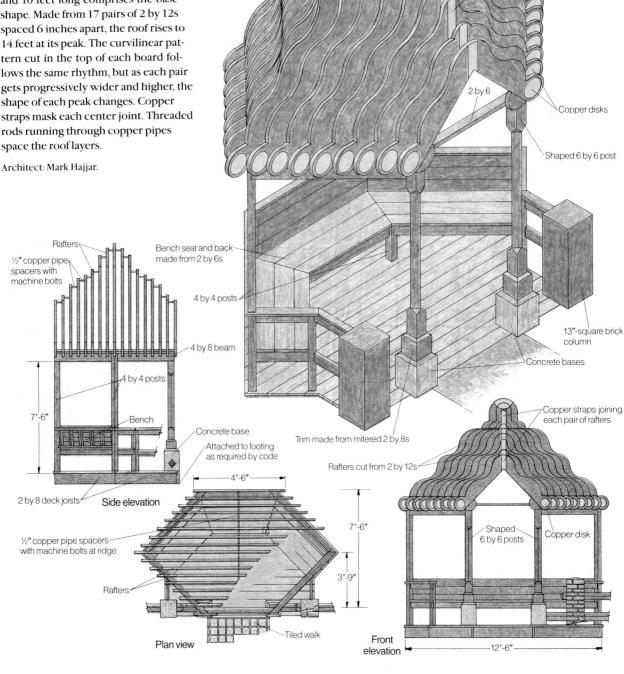

Rafters cut from 2 by 12s

Copper straps

2 by 6

Copper disks

Shaped 6 by 6 post

13"-square brick column

Concrete bases

Bench seat and back made from 2 by 6s

4 by 4 posts

Trim made from mitered 2 by 8s

Rafters

½" copper pipe spacers with machine bolts

4 by 8 beam

4 by 4 posts

Bench

Concrete base
Attached to footing as required by code

7'-6"

2 by 8 deck joists · Side elevation

½" copper pipe spacers with machine bolts at ridge

Rafters

4'-6"

Plan view

Tiled walk

7'-6"

3'-9"

Front elevation

12'-6"

Copper straps joining each pair of rafters

Rafters cut from 2 by 12s

Shaped 6 by 6 posts

Copper disk

Whimsical gazebo takes on a magical appearance at night, thanks to dramatic outdoor illumination. Photos at right show rafter and post details.

ROSE-COVERED GAZEBO

Roses climb up and over this gazebo, providing lush, colorful shade. Cut into the side of a canyon, the gazebo ties to a 5-foot retaining wall that keeps the hillside at bay. (The wall doesn't support the structure.)

Set on a 10-foot-square concrete pad, the frame is made from five sets of 2 by 12s with lapped joints; bolts through steel plates, fabricated at a welding shop, reinforce each joint. The benches' backrests and 2 bys at the top keep the frames evenly spaced.

Landscape architect: Pamela Burton, Burton & Spitz. Architect: Urban Innovations Group.

Heavy timbers make a sturdy framework for this combination trellis-gazebo, a shady retreat for family and friends.

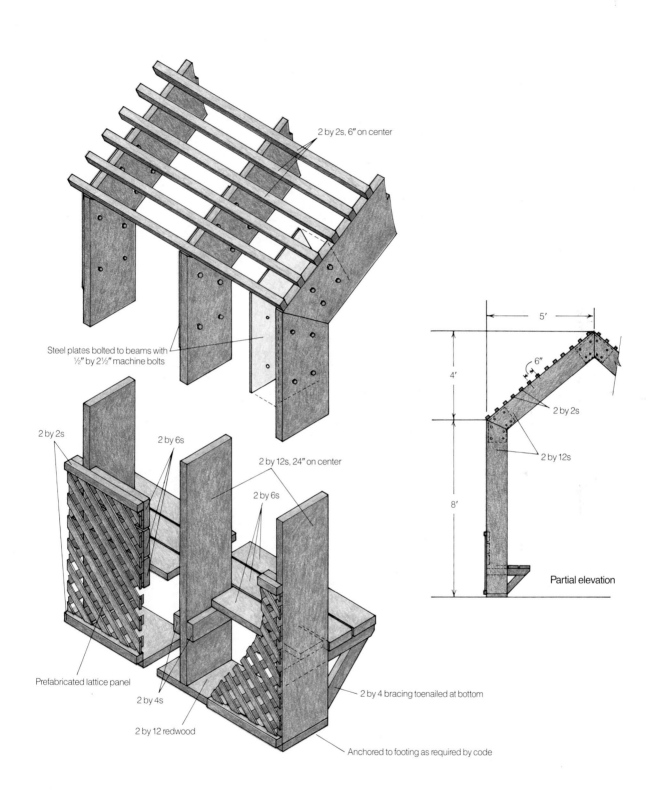

2 by 2s, 6" on center

Steel plates bolted to beams with
½" by 2½" machine bolts

2 by 2s

2 by 6s

2 by 12s, 24" on center

2 by 6s

Prefabricated lattice panel

2 by 4s

2 by 12 redwood

2 by 4 bracing toenailed at bottom

Anchored to footing as required by code

5'

6"

4'

2 by 2s

2 by 12s

8'

Partial elevation

■CORNER GAZEBO

Elegantly framing the corner of a deck, this L-shaped gazebo offers comfortable seating for casual conversation or quiet contemplation. Its charm is the result of interesting detailing and careful workmanship, evidenced in its bandsawed knee braces and mitered 2 by 2 roofing.

The 4 by 4 posts connect to the deck's substructure; decking is cut to fit around them. Latticework bench backs are actually prefabricated lattice panels. Cushions, purchased at an outdoor furniture store, soften the seats. Outdoor light fixtures fastened to the ceiling joists brighten the space for evening enjoyment.

Architect: Mark Hajjar.

Mitered 2 by 2 roofing admits light, yet still shelters gazebo from elements.

Comfortable and congenial, covered gazebo off family room perches on edge of hillside deck.

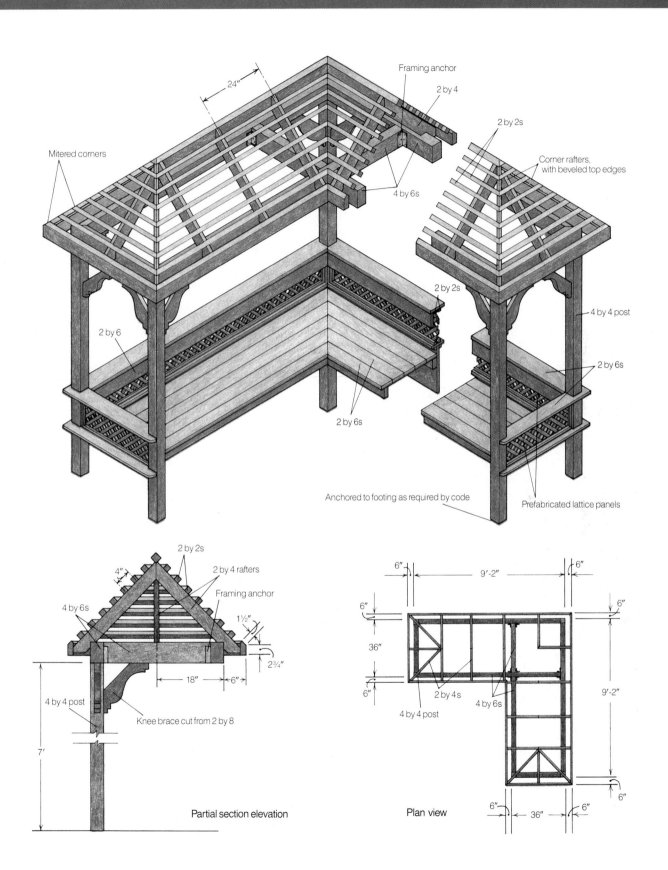

Mitered corners

24"

Framing anchor

2 by 4

2 by 2s

Corner rafters, with beveled top edges

4 by 6s

2 by 2s

4 by 4 post

2 by 6

2 by 6s

2 by 6s

Anchored to footing as required by code

Prefabricated lattice panels

2 by 2s

2 by 4 rafters

Framing anchor

4"

4 by 6s

1½"

2¾"

4 by 4 post

18"

6"

7'

Knee brace cut from 2 by 8

Partial section elevation

6"

9'-2"

6"

6"

6"

36"

6"

9'-2"

2 by 4s

4 by 6s

4 by 4 post

6"

36"

6"

6"

Plan view

BUILDING TECHNIQUES

Whether you're in the midst of developing a workable design or you're ready to start building, this chapter will serve as a helpful guide and reference for planning and building a patio roof, gazebo, or similar outdoor structure.

Beginning on the facing page, you'll learn how to select and buy lumber and fasteners. The sections that follow explain basic building techniques—from laying the foundation to nailing on the finished roof. How to add such amenities as benches and trellises is discussed on pages 92–93. The chapter concludes with instructions for finishing and caring for your outdoor structure.

It's a good idea to read through the entire chapter before beginning construction. You'll need a clear understanding of building techniques at the design stage in order to determine beam sizes, post spacings, and other important structural details.

Uprights made from four inter-locked timbers solidly support massive trellis. Semitransparent stain protects wood without obscuring its rough-sawn texture. Landscape architect: Kenneth W. Wood.

Shopping for lumber, fasteners, and other materials can be an intimidating experience. If the choices don't over-whelm you, the prices surely will. The best way to get through a lumberyard or home-improvement center with a mini-mum of confusion and expense is to know what materials to buy and how much of each you'll need.

Here is some basic information on buying the lumber and fasteners you'll need in order to construct your project.

LUMBER BUYERS GUIDE

Regardless of the material you've chosen for the roof of your outdoor structure, chances are that its framework is con-structed from wood. (For more infor-mation on the basic characteristics of the different wood products, turn to page 10.)

Choosing Lumber

Lumber is divided into softwoods and hardwoods, terms that refer to the origin of the wood. Softwoods come from con-ifers, hardwoods from deciduous trees.

As a rule, softwoods are much less expensive, easier to tool, and more read-ily available than hardwoods. In fact, nearly all outdoor construction today is done with softwoods. Hardwoods are generally reserved for fine interior finish work.

Softwoods come in a wide range of sizes and lengths, in several different fin-ishes, and in various species and grades.

Species. Woods from different trees have varying properties. Redwood, ce-dar, and cypress heartwoods (the darker part of the wood, cut from the tree's core) have a natural resistance to de-cay. This, combined with their beauty, makes them a favorite for decks, natural-finish lath-type roofing, and similar applications. But these woods can be more expensive than such ordinary structural woods as Douglas fir, yellow southern pine, and western larch.

When used for structural elements or where paint or stain will cover the wood's natural beauty, redwood and cedar can push the cost unnecessarily high. Many landscape professionals specify Douglas fir or another structural wood for those parts of an overhead. Applying a protective finish will help ensure durability (see page 94).

Lumber grades. At the mill, lumber is sorted and identified with a stamp according to quality, moisture content, grade name, and, in many cases, the species and the grading agency. Gener-ally, grade depends on natural growth characteristics (such as knots), defects resulting from milling errors, and man-ufacturing techniques in drying and pre-serving that affect the wood's strength, durability, or appearance.

Surfaced lumber, the standard for most construction, comes in nearly all grades. Rough lumber tends to be avail-able only in lower grades and has a greater number of defects and a higher moisture content.

Besides grade, it may be important to look for treated lumber, wood that's been factory-treated with preservatives that repel rot, insects, and other causes of decay. Foundation-grade pressure-treated lumber is generally the most economical, long-lasting choice for any wood that's in contact with the ground.

The American Wood Preservers Bureau (AWPB), which governs this industry, grade-stamps pressure-treated lumber; look for their stamp (shown below).

If you're not planning to buy pres-sure-treated lumber and you're not using decay-resistant wood, consider pretreating the wood with a water repellent or finish *before* construction to protect areas where pieces join.

In general, you get what you pay for. Higher grades are almost always con-siderably more expensive than lower grades. One of the best ways to save money on a project is to pinpoint the *right* grade (not necessarily the *best* grade) for each element.

How lumber is sold. Lumber is sold either by the linear foot or by the board foot. The *linear* foot, commonly used for small orders, considers only the length of a piece. For example, twenty 2 by 4s, 8 feet long, would be the same as 160 linear feet of 2 by 4.

The *board* foot is the most common unit for volume orders; lumberyards often quote prices per 1,000 board feet. A piece of wood 1 inch thick, 12 inches wide, and 12 inches long equals one board foot. To compute board feet, use this formula: thickness in inches X width in feet X length in feet. For example, a 1

Typical Grading Stamps

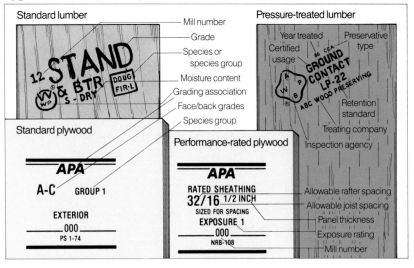

Grading stamps offer information on product quality and characteristics. APA trademark courtesy of American Plywood Association.

by 6 board 10 feet long would be computed as follows:

$$1'' \times \frac{1}{2}' \, (6'') \times 10' = 5 \text{ board feet}$$

Of course, you'll still need to list the exact dimensions of the lumber you need so your order can be filled correctly. Lumber is normally stocked in even lengths from 6 to 20 feet.

Remember that a finished 2 by 4 is not 2 inches by 4 inches. The nominal size of lumber is designated before the piece is dried and surfaced; the finished size is less. For actual sizes of nominal dimensions, see page 11.

To figure the minimum sizes you'll need to support loads, consult the tables on page 76. Note that your area's building codes may vary from those figures.

Plywood & Structural Wood Panels

In gazebo and patio roof construction, standard plywood is occasionally used for sheathing, for strengthening a structure, or for building concrete forms. Plywood and hardboard sidings may be used for roofing.

Standard plywood panels measure 4 by 8 feet; thicknesses range from ¼ to ¾ inch. Panels come in either interior or exterior grades. Be sure to specify exterior panels where the plywood will be exposed to the elements.

The appearance of a panel's face and back determines its grade. Letters A through D designate the different grades, A being the highest and D the lowest. A/C (exterior) panels are economical choices where only one side will be visible. Face and back grades, glue type, and group number should be stamped on each panel, along with an association trademark that assures quality.

Before using plywood, it's best to seal all edges with water repellent, stain sealer, or exterior house paint primer.

FASTENERS

Regardless of the type of overhead you're planning, you'll no doubt need a variety of nails, bolts or screws, and metal connectors to join materials and strengthen joints.

Nails

Nails are sold in 1-, 5-, and 50-pound boxes, or loose in bins. The term "penny" (abbreviated, oddly, as "d") indicates a nail's length. Here are equivalents in inches for the most common sizes:

4d = 1½"	5d = 1¾"	6d = 2"
7d = 2¼"	8d = 2½"	10d = 3"
12d = 3¼"	16d = 3½"	20d = 4"

Outside, use hot-dipped galvanized, aluminum, or stainless steel nails; other types will rust. In fact, even the best hot-dipped nail will rust in time, particularly at the exposed nail head where the coating is battered by your hammer. Stainless steel or aluminum nails won't rust, but they're more costly than galvanized nails. You'll probably have to special-order them.

Common nails, favored for construction, have an extra-thick shank and a broad head. Where you don't want the nail's head to show, choose a finishing nail; after you drive it nearly flush, you sink the head with a nailset.

Bolts & Lag Screws

The most rigid joint fasteners are bolts and lag screws (see illustration at right). These heavy-duty fasteners are recommended for any connection where strength is particularly important.

Bolt lengths range from 3 to 12 inches, diameters from ¼ to ¾ inch in ¹⁄₁₆-inch increments. Bolts should be approximately 1 inch longer than the thickness of the combined pieces to accommodate washers and nuts. Plan to predrill bolt holes using a drill of the same diameter as the bolt. Use washers under all nuts and under the heads of machine bolts only; the heads of carriage bolts bite into the wood, keeping the bolt from turning as you tighten the nut.

Lag screws are substitutes for bolts and come in equivalent sizes. They're particularly useful in tight spots where you can reach only one side of the connection with a wrench (a socket wrench is easiest). Plan to predrill a lead

hole about two-thirds the length of the lag screw, using a drill ⅛ inch smaller than the lag screw's shank. Place a washer under each lag screw's head.

It's better to make a connection using several small-diameter bolts or lag screws rather than fewer large-diameter bolts. The number and size will depend on the width of the lumber being joined. Typical combinations are shown below.

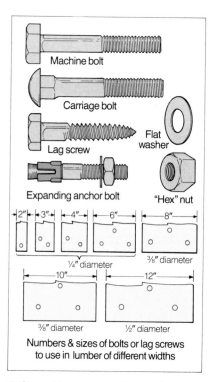

Numbers & sizes of bolts or lag screws to use in lumber of different widths

Bolts and lag screws offer sturdy, rigid fastening.

For securing ledgers to a masonry wall or anchoring posts to a slab floor, use expanding anchor bolts. They feature expanding sleeves that grip the surrounding hole firmly when the nut is driven home.

Framing Connectors

Often used in construction, metal connectors (shown on facing page) make joining materials easier; they also help strengthen joints. You'll find many types of framing connectors in sizes to fit most standard-dimension rough and surfaced lumber.

A Selection of Framing Connectors

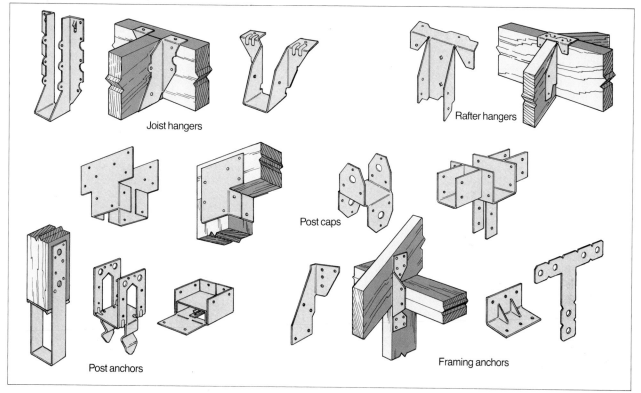

Joist hangers

Rafter hangers

Post caps

Post anchors

Framing anchors

When using framing connectors, be sure to use the size and type nail specified by the manufacturer.

Joist and rafter hangers, probably the most familiar metal connectors, are used to make secure butt joints between ceiling joists, or rafters, and the load-bearing beam, joist header, or ledger.

Post caps are used at the top of a post to join the post to a beam. They're also used to strengthen a splice connection between two beams.

Post anchors secure the base of a load-bearing post to a concrete foundation, slab, or deck. In areas where there's likely to be a lot of standing water or rain, builders typically choose an elevated post base that raises a post 1 to 3 inches above the surface.

Framing anchors may be any of a number of different connectors, both functional and decorative, made for reinforcing connections.

ESTIMATING & ORDERING MATERIALS

To reduce the cost of materials, remember these basic rules: 1) Order as much as possible at one time from one supplier, 2) choose your supplier on the basis of competitive bids from several retailers, and 3) order materials in regularly available, standard dimensions and in quantities 5 to 10 percent greater than your estimated needs.

Lumber. Carefully review your building plans, counting up pieces to develop a list of the lumber you'll need.

Roofing materials. On your plans, sketch standard *plywood panels* (if you're using them) over the framing system you've planned; then count them. To estimate *shingles* for a solid roof, you need to find the number of squares (1 square = 100 square feet) in the roof surface. To do this, multiply the roof's length by its width and then

divide the result by 100, rounding off to the next highest figure. Add 10 percent to allow for waste.

To estimate hip and ridge shingles, measure the lengths of hips and ridges, and divide the total by the exposure recommended for the shingles.

Measure the total length of eaves and rakes for *drip edge flashing* and the length of valleys for *valley flashing.*

Figure roughly 1½ pounds of *roofing nails* per square of asphalt shingles and 2 pounds per square of wood shingles or shakes. You'll also need about 2 pounds of nails for the starter course and the hip and ridge shingles.

Fasteners. Count the number of posts, beams, joists, or rafters requiring metal framing connectors. Note where bolts and screws are used and count them.

Nails are difficult to estimate. Probably the best approach is to assess your planned nailing pattern for a given unit, count up the number of nails for that unit, and multiply by the total units.

Though there are many different designs for patio roofs and gazebos, most are constructed from the same basic components—a foundation, posts or walls, beams, rafters (or joists), and some type of roofing. The typical components of both an attached patio roof and a gazebo are shown at right.

PROVIDING A SOUND FOUNDATION

Patio roofs and gazebos are typically supported by a foundation, usually a series of footings and piers. The foundation distributes a structure's weight on the ground and anchors the structure against settling, erosion, and wind lift. The foundation also isolates the posts (or walls) from direct contact with the ground, reducing the chance of decay and insect infestation.

Building codes govern the size and spacing of footings and piers and specify how deep into the ground they must go. Typically, footings must extend into solid ground or rock, and, in cold climates, below the frost line so they're not disturbed by frost heave. The spacing between footings is determined by post placements, which are controlled by beam spans (see page 76).

Sometimes, a lightweight overhead or gazebo can sit directly on a patio slab or deck without an additional foundation, depending on the slab's thickness or the deck's construction (see "Building on an Existing Slab or Deck," page 77). Again, codes determine if this support is sufficient.

A house-attached patio roof takes advantage of the house's support by connecting on one side to a horizontal ledger mounted on the house. The ledger, usually a 2 by 6, often supports one end of the patio roof rafters. The ledger should be attached before the foundation is built.

Mounting a Ledger

Locating and mounting a ledger is normally a fairly easy process—far easier than pouring footings and setting piers.

Patio Roof & Gazebo Anatomy

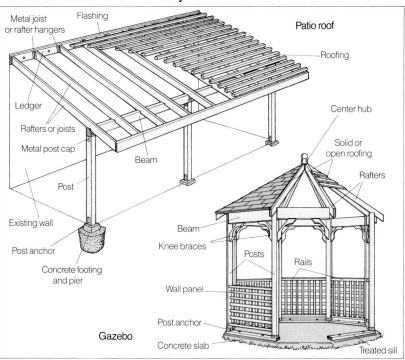

Locating the ledger. The best place to mount a ledger is on the wall under the eaves; it's fastened through the siding to the house framing. Measure first to make sure there'll be room for rafters between the ledger and eave line.

If the eaves aren't high enough to allow proper headroom, support the patio roof by mounting it on the house roof in one of the ways shown below. Don't fasten it to the eaves; it might exert undue leverage on the house rafters.

Rafter Connections for Attached Patio Roofs

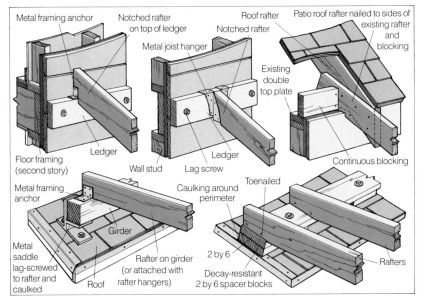

Fastening the ledger to the house. For a wood-frame (or stucco) house, the ledger must be lag-screwed to the interior framing, either to wall studs or, on a two-story house, to floor framing. Ledgers are fastened to masonry houses using expanding anchor bolts.

■ *Wood-frame house.* Lag screws securing a ledger to a wood-frame house must penetrate into interior framing members. In a one-story house, screw into wall studs, located on 16- or 24-inch centers, or, on a roof, into roof rafters. In a two-story house (shown below), look for floor framing members about 6 inches below the interior floor level.

First, level the ledger at the desired height. If the house has wood siding, you can temporarily nail the ledger in place; otherwise, just brace it securely. Then recheck for level and drill lag screw holes through the ledger and siding into studs or into floor framing. Finally, lag-screw the ledger in place every 16 inches with ½- by 5½-inch lag screws (or as

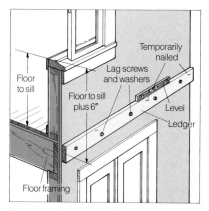

Locate ledger where it can be lag-screwed to upper floor framing for easiest and strongest connection.

specified by local codes). Recheck level as you work.

■ *Masonry walls.* To attach a ledger to masonry, first mark a line across the wall for the ledger's top edge and drill holes in the wall for expanding anchors. Insert the anchors and, holding the ledger in place, tap with a hammer to mark the anchor locations on the back face of the ledger.

Remove the ledger and drill bolt holes in it where marked. Then push (or hammer) onto the bolts, recheck level, add washers and nuts, and tighten.

■ *Flashing the ledger.* Unless it's protected from rain by the eaves or by its own solid roofing material, a ledger fastened directly to a house should be capped with galvanized metal flashing (see page 86) and caulked to prevent moisture penetration before the rafters are fastened in place.

To bend sheet metal flashing, make a form, clamping two 2 by 4s together on each side; then hammer to fold. Fit the flashing in place, as shown below, caulk the top edge, and nail it to the ledger and house siding with galvanized nails long

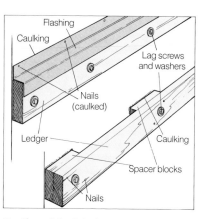

Caulk and flash ledger to prevent water damage; or mount on spacers and caulk.

enough to penetrate at least 1 inch into studs or other structural members. Caulk the nail heads.

If the house has shingled or lapped siding (or if you're fastening the ledger to the roof), you needn't caulk the top edge of the flashing. Instead, slip it up as far as possible under the bottom edge of the shingles or siding.

A less decay-resistant alternative to flashing is to set the ledger out from the house wall, using spacer blocks. Blocks are spaced at the intervals determined by bolts or lag screws.

■ *Optional support method.* Sometimes, you can cantilever short, lightweight

roofs from a house wall, eliminating the need for posts. Because of the loads exerted by cantilevered roofs, this work should be left to professionals.

Laying Out Footings

Beam and rafter spans determine post spacings. The distance a particular beam may span depends on the wood's species, the loads the beam must bear, and the beam's size and grade. Post and rafter sizes are figured the same way. The tables on page 76 show typical standards. Since these may be different from requirements in your area, be sure to check with your local building department.

Once you've determined the size and locations of your overhead's footings, carefully transfer these measurements to the ground, deck, or patio.

Ensuring square corners. If your design calls for corners that form exact 90° angles, use the 3-4-5 rule to square the corners. You'll need a helper and two tape measures.

For a house-attached overhead, drive one nail into the ledger's end and a second nail into the ledger exactly 3 feet away. Have your helper hook the end of one tape measure onto each nail; then pull out the tapes until the 4-foot mark on the tape attached to the ledger's end intersects the 5-foot mark on the other tape, as shown below.

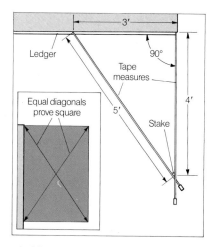

Establish "square" by creating a 3-4-5 triangle with two tape measures.

SIZING SUPPORT MEMBERS

The number, size, and spacing of rafters, beams, and posts needed for a patio roof or gazebo are determined by the loads they must carry. Loads are divided into two categories: live and dead. *Live* loads are stresses independent of a structure, such as wind, earthquake, or the weight of people. *Dead* loads are those applied by the structure itself—the rafters, roofing, and so forth. Both are measured in pounds per square foot, or "psf."

In areas with mild climates, patio roofs are generally designed for combined live and dead loads of 30 psf. In areas of heavy snowfall or winds, roofs should be based on loads of 40 to 50 psf. Call your local building department for code requirements in your area. Roofs with pitches of at least 4 in 12 (see page 85) can generally handle heavier loads than flatter roofs.

The tables here give maximum recommended spans for rafters and beams by types of wood. The figures are based on quality materials, for example, No. 2 and better. For lesser grades, spans will be shorter. Keep in mind that these are maximums—you may want to shorten them slightly for a more solid structure. You can use 4 by 4 posts for most overheads. Exceptions include very tall (over 12 feet) or heavy structures.

From Table 1, select the wood you intend to use to determine its group. Next, find out the loads your overhead must bear and then use Table 2 to choose rafter sizes that will both look good and carry the weight. Finally, look at Table 3 to figure beam placements and how best to coordinate them with rafters. Remember that beams will be supported by posts, and post placements will be critical to aesthetics and traffic flow.

TABLE 1: STRENGTH GROUPINGS OF COMMON SOFTWOODS

Group 1 (strongest)

Douglas fir
Hemlock, western
Larch, western
Pine, southern
Spruce, coast Sitka

Group 2

Cedar, western
Cypress
Douglas fir (south)
Fir (white, Alpine)
Hemlock (eastern, mountain)
Pine (eastern white, Idaho white, lodgepole, northern, Ponderosa, red, sugar, western white)
Redwood
Spruce (eastern, Engelmann, Sitka)

TABLE 2: MAXIMUM RECOMMENDED RAFTER SPANS

The following spans are based on a roof pitch of 3 in 12 or less.

Load	Rafter Size	Maximum Rafter Spacing					
		12"		16"		24"	
		Group 1	Group 2	Group 1	Group 2	Group 1	Group 2
30 psf*	2 by 4	10'-0"	9'-0"	9'-0"	8'-3"	8'-0"	7'-3"
30 psf	2 by 6	15'-9"	14'-6"	14'-3"	13'-0"	12'-6"	11'-6"
30 psf	2 by 8	20'-3"	19'-0"	18'-9"	17'-0"	16'-6"	15'-0"
50 psf	2 by 4	8'-0"	7'-3"	7'-3"	6'-6"	6'-3"	5'-9"
50 psf	2 by 6	12'-6"	11'-6"	11'-6"	10'-3"	10'-0"	9'-0"
50 psf	2 by 8	16'-6"	15'-0"	15'-0"	13'-6"	13'-0"	12'-0"

*Pounds per square foot

TABLE 3: MAXIMUM RECOMMENDED BEAM SPANS

Size	Load	Spacing between Beams (or Beam to Ledger)							
		8 feet		10 feet		12 feet		16 feet	
		Group 1	Group 2	Group 1	Group 2	Group 1	Group 2	Group 1	Group 2
2 by 6	30 psf	7'-9"	7'-0"	7'-3"	6'-6"	6'-9"	6'-3"	6'-3"	5'-6"
	50 psf	6'-0"	5'-6"	5'-9"	5'-3"				
2 by 8	30 psf	10'-3"	9'-6"	9'-6"	8'-6"	9'-0"	8'-0"	8'-3"	7'-6"
	50 psf	8'-0"	7'-6"	7'-6"	6'-9"				
2 by 10	30 psf	13'-3"	12'-0"	12'-3"	11'-3"	11'-6"	10'-6"	10'-6"	9'-6"
	50 psf	10'-6"	9'-6"	9'-9"	8'-9"				
2 by 12	30 psf	16'-0"	14'-6"	14'-9"	13'-6"	14'-0"	12'-9"	12'-9"	11'-6"
	50 psf	12'-9"	11'-6"	11'-9"	10'-9"				
4 by 4	30 psf	6'-6"	6'-0"	6'-0"	5'-6"	5'-9"	5'-3"	5'-3"	4'-9"
	50 psf	5'-3"	4'-9"	4'-6"	4'-3"				
4 by 6	30 psf	10'-3"	9'-6"	9'-6"	8'-9"	9'-0"	8'-3"	8'-3"	7'-6"
	50 psf	8'-3"	7'-6"	7'-6"	7'-0"				
4 by 8	30 psf	13'-9"	12'-6"	12'-9"	11'-6"	12'-0"	11'-0"	10'-9"	10'-0"
	50 psf	10'-9"	9'-9"	10'-0"	9'-3"				
4 by 10	30 psf	17'-6"	16'-0"	16'-3"	14'-6"	15'-3"	14'-0"	13'-9"	12'-6"
	50 psf	13'-9"	12'-6"	12'-9"	11'-9"				
4 by 12	30 psf	20'-6"	19'-6"	19'-9"	18'-3"	18'-6"	17'-0"	16'-9"	15'-6"
	50 psf	16'-9"	15'-6"	15'-6"	14'-3"				

Drive a stake into the ground (or mark the deck or patio) at this point. Measure from the ledger along the stake the required distance to establish the corner post location and drive in another stake. Repeat on the other side.

For a freestanding overhead, use the same method; just start from stakes in the ground instead of the ledger.

This triangulation method works in any multiple of 3-4-5 (for example, 6-8-10 or 9-12-15). For maximum accuracy, use the largest ratio possible.

Refining the layout. For precise placement of posts, set up batterboards. These will allow you to adjust and maintain taut perimeter lines after you've removed the layout stakes to dig the footings. Locate batterboards about 18 inches from each corner stake.

If you're building off an existing house wall, run a plumb line down from each end of the ledger and drive a nail partially into the wall at the line. Run mason's lines from the nails to the opposite batterboards and then from batterboard to batterboard, as shown below. Measure diagonally from opposite corners, adjusting the lines until the measurements are the same.

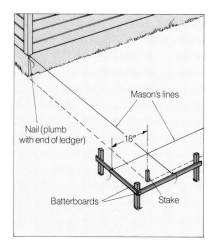

Mason's lines attached to batterboards allow for precise layout of posts.

With a level or plumb bob, plumb down from the intersections of the lines to recheck the corner stakes. Measure along the lines and plumb down to locate perimeter footings.

Fastening Posts to an Existing Slab or Deck

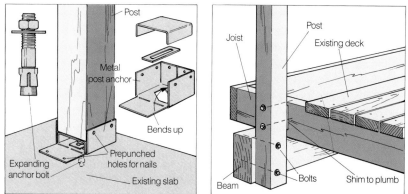

Mount post on a slab (if code approved), using a post anchor secured with an anchor bolt (at left). On an existing deck, bolt to framing (at right).

Remember that these lines show the perimeter of the posts and footings, not their centers. Make the necessary adjustments to center the footings.

Building on an Existing Slab or Deck

If your overhead will cover an existing patio or deck, consider whether the patio or deck can support the overhead without additional foundation work. Depending on the overhead's weight and the thickness of the slab (or the construction of the deck), codes may allow setting the overhead directly on the slab or deck, as explained below.

If the slab isn't thick enough or the overhead is too heavy, you'll have to either pour new footings around the slab's perimeter or break out sections and pour deeper footings.

Building over an existing slab. To fasten an overhead directly to an existing slab, you'll have to secure each post in a post anchor like the one shown above. Post anchors are made for both rough and surfaced 4 by 4, 4 by 6, and 6 by 6 posts. (For other sizes, you may need to have anchors specially fabricated.)

Using a masonry bit, drill a hole, centered for each anchor, to receive a ½-inch expanding anchor bolt. Insert the bolt, add the post anchor, and then follow up with a washer and nut. Tighten

the connection. When it's time to add the post, you just cut the end square, place it in the stirrup of the post anchor, and nail the plate to the post.

Building over an existing deck. Posts can be bolted or lag-screwed to the sides of existing deck beams, joists, rafters, or other heavy structural members. Or you can use the post bases discussed above, lag-screwing them through decking to a joist or beam.

Setting Footings & Piers

Typically, posts rest on piers embedded in poured concrete footings. There are three different methods for building a foundation: you can pour the footings and piers at the same time; you can place ready-made piers into wet concrete footings; or you can bond ready-made piers to dry concrete footings.

Preparing footings. Dig an appropriately sized hole in the ground deep enough to allow for about 6 inches of gravel beneath the concrete. Before adding the gravel, tamp the bottom of the hole and add any necessary steel reinforcing bar (normally required if piers are more than a foot high or if only a few are used). Plan to fill the hole with fresh concrete to within about 6 inches of ground level.

For small amounts, you can buy premixed bagged concrete and add water,

Two Ways to Set Piers

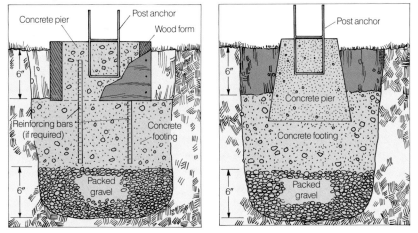

Before concrete footing sets up, either form and pour a contiguous pier (at left), or position and level a ready-made pier (at right).

though it's generally less expensive to mix your own. For large amounts, have the concrete delivered.

To mix your own concrete, use 1 part cement, 2 parts clean river sand, and 3 parts gravel (maximum of 1 inch in diameter and specially washed for concrete mixing). Add clean water, a little at a time, as you mix. The concrete should be plastic but not runny.

When mixing concrete, pay special attention to the ratio of water to cement. Concrete hardens because the powder-like cement and water form an adhesive that binds the sand and gravel. Too much water thins or dilutes this paste and weakens its cementing qualities; too little makes it stiff and unworkable.

You can use a shovel or hoe to mix the concrete on a wood platform or in a wheelbarrow. Spread two shovelsful of sand and one of cement on the mixing surface. Using the shovel in a rolling motion, mix until the color is even. Then add three shovelsful of gravel and continue mixing for even color. Finally, scoop out a hole in the middle of the dry ingredients and add 3 quarts of water.

Work around the puddle, slowly rolling the dry ingredients into the water. Take particular care not to slop the water out of the wheelbarrow.

If the batch is too stiff, add water, a cup at a time, and continue mixing until it's right. If the mixture is too soupy, add small amounts of sand and gravel (concrete at this stage of mixing changes consistency radically when you add even small amounts of ingredients).

If you're using a machine-powered mixer, estimate the 1:2:3 proportions of cement, sand, and gravel by shovelsful. Add 2½ gallons of water per half-bag of cement. Tumble for 2 or 3 minutes and then pour.

Making forms for piers. If you're planning to pour piers and footings together, you'll need to make forms for the piers before you can pour the concrete. You can use either scrap wood (for large piers, you'll need to twist lengths of wire around the perimeter) or old 3- to 5-gallon cans with tops and bottoms cut out. (Preslit the sides and hold them in shape with wire to simplify removing them later on.)

For cylindrical piers, use specially manufactured fiber tube forms. These tubes can be sawed to any length and have a coated inner surface that makes peeling them off later an easy job.

Pouring contiguous footings and piers. Pour the footings first. Then place and level the piers' forms over the wet concrete footings, inserting any steel reinforcing required to strengthen the link between footings and piers (see illustration above, at left).

Fill the forms with concrete, using a screed or straight board to level the wet concrete flush with the tops of the forms. Immediately embed metal post anchors (see page 73). While the concrete is still plastic, hold a carpenter's level against a short length of post placed in the post anchors to check for plumb.

Keeping the piers damp, leave the forms on the piers for at least a week while the concrete cures. If the piers are exposed to direct sun or hot, dry weather during this time, cover them with newspapers, straw, or burlap sacks and keep moist so they'll dry slowly.

Using ready-made piers on wet concrete. Ready-made piers are available with either wooden nailing blocks or integral metal post anchors. Opt for the latter—posts will be more secure fastened to the metal anchors.

Soak the piers well with a hose before positioning them. Place them on the footings 5 to 10 minutes after the footings have been poured. Then check for level.

Bonding ready-made piers to dry footings. Drench the top of each footing and the bottom of each pier with water. Then, using a creamy cement paste, coat both surfaces ½ to 1 inch thick. Set each pier in place on the footings. Check to be sure the top of each pier is level.

POSTS & BEAMS

In typical patio roof construction, beams run from post to post (sometimes from post to ledger). The beams support the roof rafters or joists, which, in turn, hold the roofing material.

Posts and columns. Posts are generally made from solid lumber, built-up lumber, steel, or a combination. In some cases, columns take the place of posts. Columns may be made from concrete, wood framing and plaster, telephone poles, or a similar material.

Wherever posts or columns will touch the ground, be sure the wood

Types of Posts & Columns

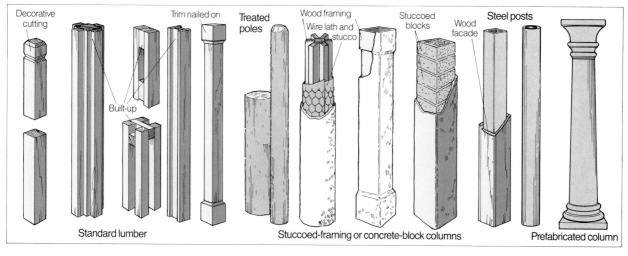

Standard lumber

Stuccoed-framing or concrete-block columns

Prefabricated column

is pressure-treated or decay-resistant. Note: Metal post anchors that raise posts about an inch off the ground allow the use of standard lumber for posts, though it's a good idea to seal the posts' ends.

For a look at some typical posts and columns, see the drawing above.

Beams. Beams, or girders, may be solid lumber or built-up lengths of 2-by dimension lumber fastened together. A built-up beam (see below) is the simplest to handle. A single, solid beam may be preferable where highly visible.

bottom edges; or bolt or lag-screw the pieces as shown.

If you must use shorter lengths to assemble a long beam, stagger the joints between successive layers; when the beam is installed, these joints must be located over a post. Be sure the crowns, the slight outward bows, on the pieces are aligned on the same side. When you mount the beam on the posts, place it crown side up.

Post and beam design. The design of beams and posts is interrelated: the

depth and thickness of the beam is determined by its span, the size and placement of the posts below, and the load of the structure above — all details specified by your building department.

Often, posts are designed to capture beams in interesting configurations, as shown below.

Posts offer plenty of latitude for detailing. You can rout them, cut them, build up interesting profiles, or nail on decorative pieces that add visual interest. For ideas, see the project section and the illustration below.

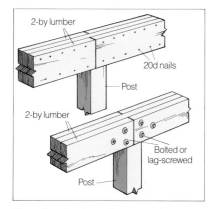

To make a built-up beam, nail together lengths of 2-by lumber (top); or bolt or lag-screw them (bottom).

The typical built-up beam consists of three thicknesses of 2-by lumber. Nail the pieces together with 20d nails spaced 3 inches apart along the top and

Post & Beam Connections

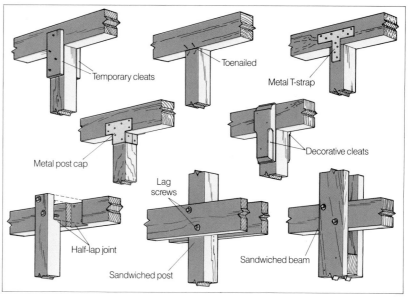

Measuring, Marking & Cutting Posts

Accurately measuring post heights is an all-important phase in building an overhead: you can't achieve a stable substructure without precise measurements and fittings. The construction examples here are for attached overheads that have both beams and rafters; if your design is different, adjust the directions accordingly.

For an attached overhead, work first on the posts farthest from the house. For a freestanding roof, begin working on the posts that support opposite edges and corners of the overhead; then do any intermediate posts.

Measuring posts for a freestanding roof differs in only one respect from measuring for an attached roof: with the attached roof, you've already defined the roof height at the ledger line; for a freestanding overhead, you'll need to erect a post slightly taller than the desired height, mark the height you wish on that post, and work from it as you would from a ledger.

Don't forget to allow for runoff from a solid or other type of roof where this is a consideration. Many roofing materials require pitch (see page 85) in order to shed rain effectively. Remember that minimum vertical clearance to the underside of a beam is normally 6 feet 8 inches.

Measuring and marking posts. Cut posts 6 to 12 inches longer than estimated finish length. Starting with the first post, have a helper hold it firmly in place on its anchor and plumb it, using a carpenter's level (check two adjacent sides). Stretch a string fitted with a line level from where the rafters' bottom edges will connect to the ledger. When the string is level, mark the post, as shown above, at left.

From that mark subtract the thickness (actual, not nominal dimension) of any beam that will sit between the post and rafter. Also subtract any necessary drop for roof pitch. Make a new mark and, with a combination square, carry it around the post's perimeter. This is your cutting line. Repeat for remaining posts.

Marking & Setting Posts

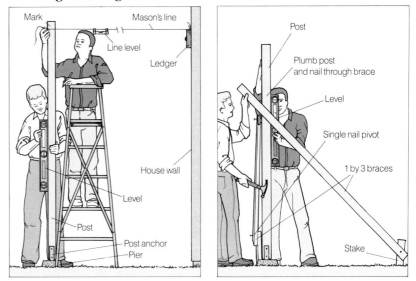

Establish post height with a line level, allowing, if necessary, for beam height and roof pitch (at left). After cutting post, brace it in position and plumb along adjacent sides (at right).

Cutting posts. Use a circular saw or handsaw to cut the posts to length. Before permanently erecting them, seal the cut ends and consider finishing the posts (see page 94).

Raising Posts

Posts can be quite heavy—you may need a helper for this work. Note: If your design calls for metal post-and-beam connectors, attach them to the posts before raising them.

Before moving the first post into position, drive stakes into the ground and nail a brace made from a 1 by 2 or 1 by 3 to each stake (use only one nail so the brace can pivot). Position the stakes far enough away from the end of the post so the braces can reach midway up the post at a 45° angle, as shown above, at right.

Seat the post squarely in its anchor and check for plumb, using a carpenter's level on adjacent sides or a plumb bob mounted on a corner. Nail the braces to the post, making sure the post is still plumb. Then nail or lag-screw the post to its base. Finally, drive additional nails into each brace to secure the posts until the beams are seated.

Seating Beams

Hoisting a large beam atop a post that stands over your head may demand more strength and agility than you possess. Be sure to get help for this stage of the construction.

There are several ways to fasten a beam to a post, as shown in the illustration on the bottom of page 79. The method described here works for post-and-beam configurations where the beam sits on top of the post. For sandwiched posts and beams or for other specialty designs, you'll have to modify these directions.

If you're not using metal post-and-beam connectors, nail a pair of wooden cleats to the supporting posts' tops, as shown at the bottom of page 79.

After cutting a beam to the proper length and finishing it (see page 94), drag it into rough position alongside the posts and slip a short length of 2 by 4 under one end. Raise that end of the beam, maneuvering it into the cradle. Partially drive in one nail so the beam won't slide off the post when the other end is lifted. Raise the other end in the same way. Finish fastening the beam to the posts.

Bracing Posts & Beams

Unless they have a steel or engineered structure, patio roofs, particularly free-standing ones, normally require cross bracing for lateral stability. For roofs less than 12 feet high, usually only outside posts on unattached sides need cross bracing. Use 2 by 4s for bracing across distances less than 8 feet, 2 by 6s for greater distances. As shown in the illustration below, you can make cross braces, or knee braces, that add a decorative element to the structure.

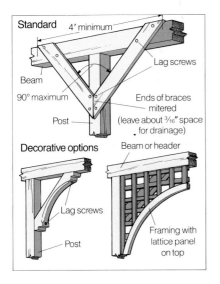

Mark individual cross braces in position and cut them on the ground. Nail them in place temporarily. Then drill pilot holes for lag screws or bolts into posts and beams, and permanently fasten them.

INSTALLING RAFTERS

Most patio roof and gazebo designs have roof rafters, or joists, of one kind or another. Rafters spread roofing loads across beams, making it possible to use thin roofing materials that otherwise couldn't span the distances between beams.

Patio roof rafters perform a double task: they must support their own weight over open space without sagging or twisting, and they must also support the added weight of the roof covering.

Rafter connections. Rafter connections can be made in several ways, as shown below. Note that rafters can

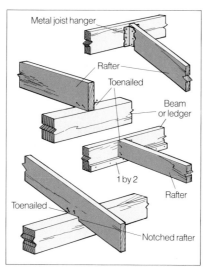

either sit on top of beams and ledgers or connect to the faces of those supports.

Gazebo hubs. Most gazebos have a center point where roof rafters meet. To join the rafter ends, which are often cut at

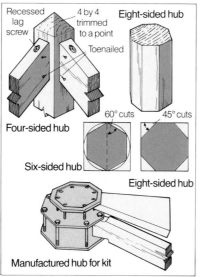

compound angles, a hub is used. Typical hubs are shown above.

Splicing rafters. Where appearance allows, rafters can be spliced with board lumber "gusset plates." To do this, the ends of the rafters are butted together over a supporting beam. Then two

pieces of 1-by lumber of the same width as the rafters and about 18 inches long are nailed on both sides of the splice. Or you can join the members using manufactured metal splice plates.

Be sure each rafter end bears a full inch on the supporting member. If several spliced rafters are needed, plan to stagger the splices over different beams to avoid weakening the substructure.

Another splicing method for rafters—though it breaks up uniform spacing—is to overlap rafter ends supported by beams. If more than one splice is needed on a full rafter length, alternate overlapped sides.

For standard 2-inch lumber, nail both faces of each splice with six 8d or 10d common galvanized nails. This type of splicing adds lateral stability to the rafter system and may eliminate the need for bracing (see page 82).

Decorative rafter cutting. Cutting rafter ends decoratively, as shown below, allows you to express your creativity and gives the patio roof a distinctive style. You'll see many examples of decorative rafter-end

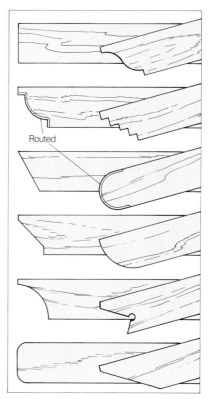

Cutting Sloping Rafters

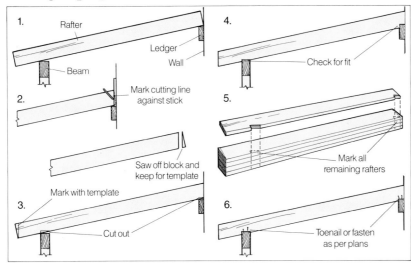

1. **Lay** a rafter so it rests on edge on both the beam and ledger.

2. **Force** the tip snugly against the house wall; then, using a straight stick as a ruler, mark the end for cutting.

3. **Cut** the triangular piece off the rafter end where it rests on the ledger strip and on the beam, as shown, and notch the beam and ledger.

4. **Cut** out the notches and position the rafter to see if it fits; check the fit in several other positions along the beam's length.

5. **Using** the rafter as a template, mark and cut the rest.

6. **Finish** the rafters (see page 94); then fasten them in place.

treatments throughout this book; one is shown below. You'll need a power saw to make most of these cuts.

Cutting and fitting sloping rafters. Fitting sloping rafters in place can be tricky for a novice. Probably the best method to use is to cut one rafter to fit and then use it as a template for the rest. The following procedure, illustrated above, tells how to cut sloping rafters for a house-attached patio roof.

Bracing Rafters

Long rafter (or joist) spans and wide spacing may result in twisted or buckled rafters, unless they're cross braced. The width of the rafters is also a consideration: those made from 2 by 8s or larger lumber require more blocking than those made from 2 by 6s. Blocking is typically determined by local codes.

Two common methods are illustrated below. If rafter spans are less than 8 feet, headers nailed across rafter ends are adequate.

Decoratively cut rafter tails, embellished with copper circles, add interest to structure. For other views of this project, turn to page 65. Architect: Mark Hajjar.

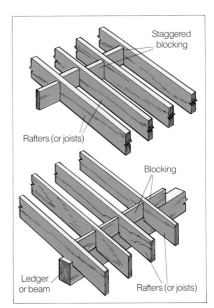

Rafters (or joists) often require blocking to prevent twisting and add strength.

Some roofing materials, such as lath, lattice panels, and other open-style roofing, are easily installed by do-it-yourselfers. Others, particularly those meant to shed rain, can be more of a challenge. Still others—glass (and some plastics), steel, tar-and-gravel, and tile —are best left to professionals.

In this section you'll find information on roofing with lath and battens, boards, louvers, asphalt shingles, asphalt roll roofing, wood shingles and shakes, solid-board and plywood siding materials, and plastic and aluminum panels. The characteristics of all the various roofing materials are discussed beginning on page 10.

The illustration below shows the anatomy of a typical house roof. Though many patio roofs are much simpler—without valleys, hips, or ridges, for example—a complex patio or gazebo roof could include any or all of these features.

OPEN-STYLE ROOFING

Open-style roofing includes a broad range of patio roof styles—designs that block the sun, frame a view, or create a feeling of enclosure, but that don't nec-essarily shed rain. Though the materials used for open-style roofing can range from thin latticework to bulky beams, the installation techniques for the various types are similar.

Roofing with Lath, Battens & Boards

Whether you're using lath, battens, boards, or even larger lumber, the width of the pieces and the spacing between them will determine the effect created by your overhead.

Creating shade. Since there are a number of variables involved, the surest way to decide on the best width, spacing, and direction of the wood is to experiment. Temporarily nail several different sizes at various spacings to the rafters and study the effects of each configuration at different times during the day.

■ *Wood thickness and spacing* can vary enormously. If you plan to use ⅜-inch-thick lath laid flat and spaced 3 inches apart, the lath won't throw much shadow. But 2 by 2s spaced half an inch apart —or 1 by 3s on edge—will cast considerable shade, as shown at right.

Here are some guidelines used by landscape architects to figure spacing.

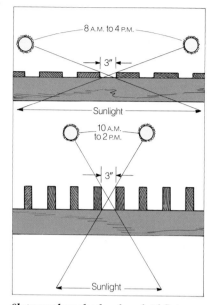

Slats cast less shade when laid flat (top) than when set on edge (bottom).

For lath up to ½ inch thick, the spacing should be from ⅜ to ¾ inch. For stock from ½ inch to 1⅛ inches thick, the spacing should be between ¾ inch and 1 inch. For 2 by 2s, the boards can be up to 2 inches apart under some circumstances, but spacing them 1 inch to 1½ inches apart will make the patio more comfortable in most cases.

■ *Direction* for running the boards is best determined by the time of day you need maximum shade. If you want the greatest relief from sun at noon, plan to run the material east-west; if you want more shade in the early morning and late afternoon, run it north-south.

■ *Roof height* affects the degree of light that falls on your patio or deck. The higher the patio roof, the more diffused the light becomes. The lower the roof, the sharper the striped shadows on your surface.

Suitable spans. To avoid sagging and warping, be conservative on the distance the wood must span. For common lath and batten, 2 feet is the maximum; with 1-inch stock, you can span up to 3 feet, but 2 feet is better; with 1- by 2-inch stock laid on edge and with 2 by 2s, you can span 4 feet without objectionable

Typical Roof Anatomy

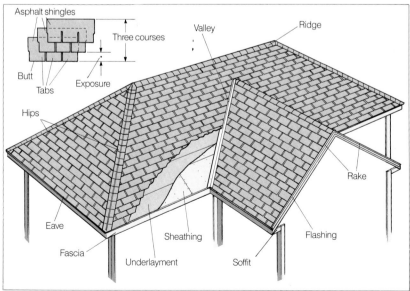

sagging, but boards may warp or curve a bit. Don't exceed 4 feet with any size.

Sight down lumber to check for any crown; when possible, face it upward.

Nailing. Though a little bit of twisting or bending is acceptable, be sure that boards are evenly spaced and in perfect alignment before you nail them.

Always use corrosion-resistant nails to secure the wood to the framework. With ⅜- or ½-inch-thick lath, use 3d or 4d common or box nails. For 1-inch stock, choose 8d nails. Use 12d or 16d nails for thicker materials. Nail twice at each rafter and join cut ends directly over rafters. If your nails split the wood, predrill nail holes.

Preassembly. To reduce the time you need to spend on the rooftop, you may want to premake panels and fasten them as shown below. Of course, you can make the panels in practically any size,

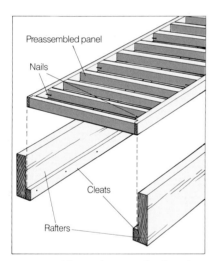

Preassemble roofing panels; then fasten them to cleats nailed to rafters.

but 3 by 6 feet is close to the optimum for lightweight material. Just be sure the structural framing is true enough to receive the panels without a struggle.

Louvered Slat Roofing

Angled louvers made from battens or boards offer an extra element of sun control. Adjustable types can give you almost any degree of light or shade you

want throughout the day; fixed louvers can block the sun during the part of the day when it's unwanted.

Louver orientation. Generally speaking, if you run louvers east-west, slanting the boards away from the sun, you'll block the midday sun and may admit morning and afternoon sun. If you run them north-south, you'll admit either morning or afternoon sun, depending on the louvers' slant.

Since the louvered overhead is designed to block direct light for part of the day, you'll have to take into account the height of the summer sun at that time. (See page 7 for information on seasonal sun angles.)

As shown below, the more you tilt the boards, the fewer pieces you'll need.

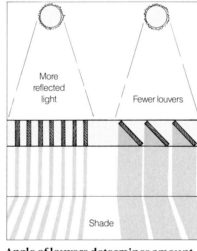

Angle of louvers determines amount of reflected light admitted and number needed.

But if you try to spread them too far, you'll diminish the amount of reflected light that can shine through.

For a pitched roof, don't forget to add the angle of the pitch to the angle of the sun's altitude when figuring louvers.

Installing fixed louvers. Fixed louvers can be built in place—nailed directly to rafters—or they can be built in modular sections and then fastened in place. The illustration above, at right, shows three different ways of fastening louvers to their supports. If you cut stepped rafters,

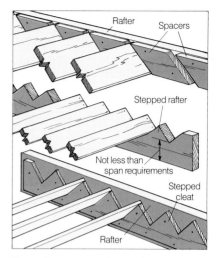

Fasten louvers to rafters using spacers, stepped rafters, or stepped cleats.

be sure their widths *measured through the depth of the cut* are not less than those specified for the span.

For the louvers, 1 by 3s, 1 by 4s, or 1 by 6s not more than 4 feet long are usually best (the narrower the pieces, the closer they'll have to be spaced).

Installing adjustable louvers. Though adjustable louvers can be exacting to build, they offer excellent sun control. If you don't want to attempt the precision work involved in making adjustable louvers, consider buying a ready-made system.

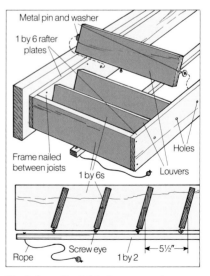

Modular adjustable-louver system offers maximum sun control.

Shown at the bottom of the facing page is one design for building your own system. Build the modules separately and then fasten them between rafters. Louvers should not exceed 4 feet in length; cut them slightly shorter than the spacing between rafters. For metal pins, aluminum nails with the heads clipped off work well.

SOLID ROOFING

There are several solid roofing materials the do-it-yourselfer can install on a patio roof or gazebo. The materials include asphalt shingles and roll roofing, wood shingles and shakes, some siding materials, and plastic or aluminum panels.

It's important to consider roof pitch when choosing your roofing material. Additionally, you may have to apply underlayment and sheathing before you can install the roofing material.

Roof Pitch

Roof pitch refers to the vertical rise measured against a standard horizontal distance of 12 inches (see illustration below). The term "4 in 12," applied to a

Two Types of Sheathing

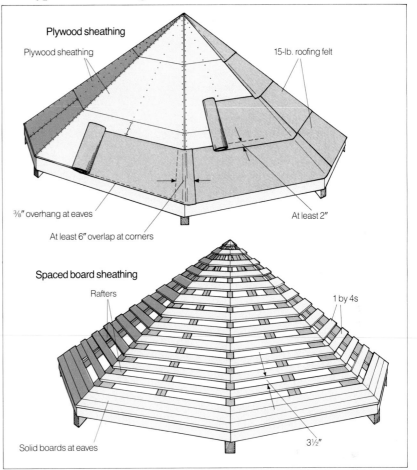

Plywood sheathing

Plywood sheathing

15-lb. roofing felt

$\frac{3}{8}$″ overhang at eaves

At least 2″

At least 6″ overlap at corners

Spaced board sheathing

Rafters

1 by 4s

Solid boards at eaves

$3\frac{1}{2}$″

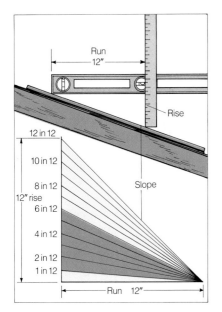

Run 12″

Rise

12 in 12

10 in 12

8 in 12

12″ rise

6 in 12

Slope

4 in 12

2 in 12

1 in 12

Run 12″

Roof pitch measures rise, in inches, for every 12 inches in run.

roof, tells you that the roof rises vertically 4 inches for every 12 horizontal inches. Very low-sloped roofs measure only 1 in 12 or 2 in 12; steeply sloped roofs range from 12 in 12 (a 45° angle) up to 20 in 12. Ordinarily, a do-it-yourselfer can work safely on roofs with slopes up to 6 in 12.

The steeper a roof's pitch, the more likely it is that water will roll off without penetrating. Asphalt shingles and wood shingles and shakes are designed for roofs with a 4 in 12 or greater slope. With additional underlayment, asphalt shingles can be applied to 2 in 12 slopes and wood shingles and shakes to 3 in 12 slopes.

Do-it-yourself plastic and aluminum panels work well on slopes as gradual as 2 in 12, asphalt roll roofing on slopes of 1 in 12 or greater.

Sheathing & Underlayment

On house roofs, asphalt shingles are normally applied over a solid deck of plywood sheathing with an underlayment of 15-pound roofing felt. Wood shakes, too, are often laid over solid decking, though in many instances they're placed over spaced 1 by 4 boards. Wood shingles are typically laid atop spaced decking. Both applications are shown above.

Patio roofs and gazebos differ from most house roofs in that, when you're looking up from underneath, most don't have ceilings to hide the structure. For that reason, solid sheathing is typically preferred. In fact, you may want to choose a higher grade material than standard sheathing; the material should have a good, paintable side or resawn texture that can be faced downward.

Solid plywood sheathing. Though some codes permit using plywood as thin as ⅜ inch on roofs, you'll probably want either ½- or ⅝-inch sheathing for a sturdier nailing base.

Stagger the sheathing horizontally across rafters, centering panel ends on rafters (leave ⅛ inch between edges and ¹⁄₁₆ inch between ends of adjoining panels for expansion). Use 6d common or box nails for plywood up to ½ inch thick, 8d nails for plywood ⅝ inch and thicker. Space nails every 6 inches along the ends of each panel and every 12 inches at intermediate supports.

Rolling out underlayment. If you're using asphalt shingles or certain other materials, you'll need to cover the decking with roofing felt. To evenly align rows of underlayment, measure the roof carefully and snap horizontal chalklines before you begin. Snap the first line 33⅝ inches above the eave (this allows for a ⅜-inch overhang). Then, providing for a 2-inch overlap between strips of felt, snap each succeeding chalkline at 34 inches.

When applying felt, start at the eave and roll the strips out horizontally along the roof, working toward the ridge or top edge. The felt should be trimmed flush at the gable overhang and overlapped 6 inches at any ridges, hips, or valleys. Where two strips meet in a vertical line, overlap them 4 inches.

Drive just enough roofing nails or staples to hold the felt in place until the roofing material is applied.

Installing spaced sheathing. For spaced sheathing, lay well-seasoned 1 by 4 boards horizontally along the roof, using another 1 by 4 as a spacing guide. Fasten each board to the rafters with two 8d nails, allowing ⅛-inch spacing where boards meet. Start your installation with solid rows of 1 by 4s at the eaves and rakes.

Flashings

Flashings protect your roof at its most vulnerable points: where the roof connects to the house, along eaves, in valleys, or anywhere water might seep into

Typical Roof Flashings

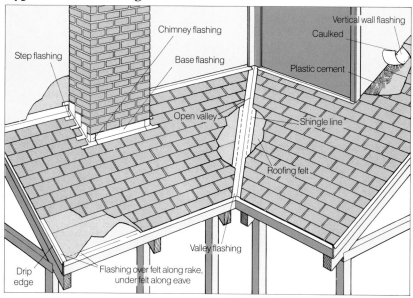

the sheathing. Flashings are most commonly made from malleable, 28-gauge galvanized sheet metal. On asphalt-shingle roofs, valleys may also be flashed with roll roofing. Plastic and aluminum flashings are used, too.

You can either buy preformed flashings for drip edges and valleys or make your own. Typical flashings are shown above. Use roofing nails to fasten them in place, positioning the nails where roofing or adjoining flashing will cover them. Caulk any exposed nail heads.

Applying Asphalt Shingles

Asphalt shingles are applied over a solid deck of plywood sheathing with an underlayment of 15-pound roofing felt. Standard three-tab shingles measure 12 by 36 inches. Most have a self-sealing mastic that welds one shingle tab to another when the shingles are installed.

The correct weather exposure for most asphalt shingles is 5 inches, meaning that the lower 5 inches of each shingle will be exposed to the weather after overlapping courses are applied.

Cutting and nailing. To cut shingles, use a utility knife to score the backs along a carpenter's square or straightedge; bend the shingles to break them.

Choose nails that won't poke through the underside of the sheathing; typically, 12-gauge, 1¼-inch-long galvanized roofing nails with ⅜-inch-diameter heads are used. When nailing, drive the heads snug with the surface, but be careful not to break the shingle's surface.

Starter course and first course. A narrow starter row of shingles runs the length of the eave to form a base for the first full course of shingles.

First, measure the eave and select enough 36-inch-long shingles to cover the distance. Then cut 3 inches off the tabs of the shingles (assuming they're 12 inches wide) so you can apply a starter course that's 9 inches wide.

Starting at the left rake, apply the starter course along the eave, placing the shingles' self-sealing strips down; trim 6 inches off the first shingle's length so the cutouts in the starter and first courses will be offset.

Allowing a ½-inch overhang at both the eave and rake and a ¹⁄₁₆-inch gap between shingles, fasten the shingles, right sides up, to the deck, using four nails placed 3 inches above the eave. Position the nails 1 inch and 12 inches in from each end.

Use full-width shingles for the first course, allowing the same ½-inch over-

Asphalt Shingle Roofing

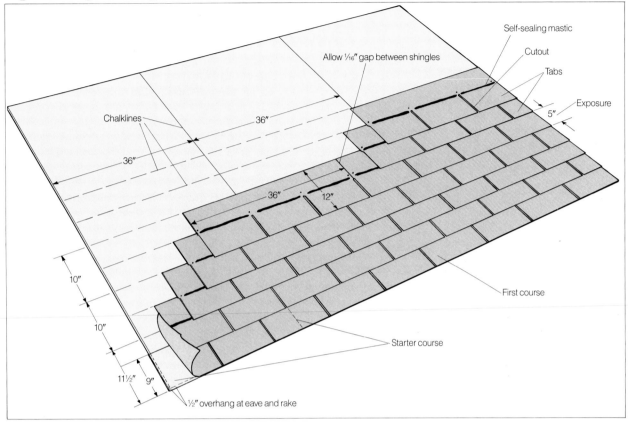

Chalklines

Allow 1/16" gap between shingles

Self-sealing mastic

Cutout

Tabs

Exposure

5"

36"

36"

36"

12"

10"

10"

11½"

9"

½" overhang at eave and rake

First course

Starter course

hang at the rake and eave and 1/16 inch between shingles. Nail the first course right on top of the starter course, using four nails for each shingle. Place the nails 5⅝ inches from the top of the shingle, and 1 and 12 inches in from each end (or according to the manufacturer's instructions).

Successive courses. Your main concern when you lay successive courses is proper alignment of the shingles — both horizontally and vertically.

Aligning shingles horizontally is simply a matter of snapping chalklines across the deck. Snap them every 10 inches from the bottom of the first course, as the drawing above shows. Then, as you move toward the ridge, the upper edge of every other course of shingles should line up with the chalklines.

Also snap vertical chalklines from the roof ridge to one end of every shingle along the first course.

Apply successive courses using the alignment of your choice. In a centered alignment, the cutouts of every other course are aligned; in a diagonal alignment, the cutouts run diagonally down the roof; and in a random alignment, the cutouts follow no particular pattern. Simply adjust the length of the shingle beginning each course to set the pattern.

Installing hip and ridge shingles. Rather than buy ready-made hip and ridge shingles, you can cut 12-inch squares from standard shingles. Bend each square to conform to the roof ridge. (In cold weather, warm the shingles before bending them.) Snap a chalkline the length of the ridge and each hip, 6 inches from the center.

If your roof has hips, start there. Beginning with a double layer of shingles at the bottom of the hip, work toward the ridge, leaving a 5-inch exposure. The edge of each shingle should line up with your chalk mark. Use

two nails, one on each side, 5½ inches from the bottom edge and 1 inch in from the outside edge (see drawing below).

To shingle a ridge, start at the end opposite the prevailing wind. Nail on the shingles in the same way as described for the hips. Caulk the exposed nail heads of the last shingle.

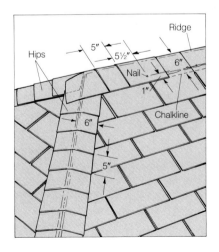

Hips

Ridge

5"

5½"

Nail

6"

1"

Chalkline

6"

5"

Using Asphalt Roll Roofing

Asphalt roll roofing, though not the most attractive, is one of the easiest and fastest roofing materials to install. Rolls of 36-inch-wide asphalt roofing are applied directly over sheathing, with the 17-inch-wide strip of mineral surface exposed and the 19-inch-wide selvage, or uncoated portion, underneath. Each layer is bonded to the next with plastic roofing cement.

Starter strip and first strip. Start with a 19-inch-wide strip long enough to cover the distance from rake to rake (cut the strip from the roll using a utility knife and straightedge). If you must join two lengths, fasten one end to the roof with nails spaced every 4 inches (1 inch from the edge); then lap and cement the adjoining end to the first (see illustration below).

Allowing a ½-inch overlap at the eave and rake, lay the starter strip along the eave and fasten it to the deck with three rows of nails spaced 12 inches apart. (Use 12-gauge, 1-inch-long galvanized nails with ⅜-inch-diameter heads; make sure nails don't poke through the sheathing.) Place the nails 4¾ inches from the upper edge, 4 inches above the bottom edge, and along the middle between them, staggering them.

Spread plastic roofing cement of a brushable consistency over the starter sheet. (Be careful not to apply too much cement, or it will ooze onto the surface when the next layer is applied.)

Finally, overlay a 36-inch-wide sheet and nail it along the top (uncoated) 19-inch portion; place the nails in two rows, the first 4¾ inches below the upper edge and the second 8½ inches below the first row of nails.

Successive strips. Bond each layer of roll roofing together with cement in the manner just described, continuing toward the ridge. Take care to seal vertical seams and to apply the proper amount of cement.

Finishing hips and ridges. Cut enough 12- by 36-inch rectangles to cover any hips and ridges. Also cut enough 12- by 17-inch rectangles so you can double the starter shingles at each hip and ridge. Then snap a chalkline the length of the hip or ridge 5½ inches from the edge.

Bend pieces lengthwise and, starting at the bottom of the hips or at the end of the ridge opposite the prevailing wind, fasten them as shown below, at left. The upper, 19-inch portion of each shingle is fastened to the roof with nails placed every 4 inches, 1 inch in from the outside edge. The lower, 17-inch portion is cemented in place.

Applying Wood Shingles & Shakes

When applying either shingles or shakes, always position the tapered ends uproof, the thicker ends downroof. Straight-split shakes (those equally thick throughout) are applied with the smooth ends uproof. If the wood has a sawn side and a rough side, install the pieces with the rough sides exposed to the weather.

Exposure. Correct exposure for wood shingles and shakes depends on their length and the slope of your roof. Recommended exposures are shown in the chart below.

Asphalt Roll Roofing

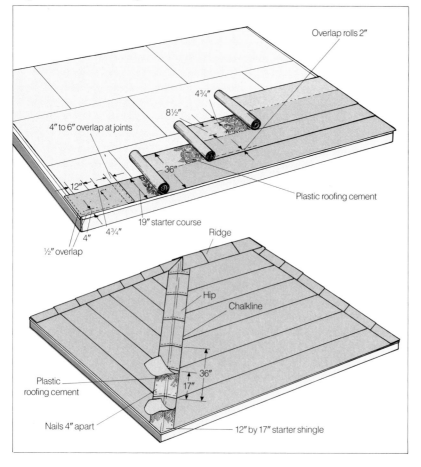

	3 in 12 to 4 in 12 slopes	4 in 12 and steeper slopes
MAXIMUM EXPOSURE FOR WOOD SHINGLES & SHAKES		
Shingles		
16"	3¾"	5"
18"	4¼"	5½"
24"	5¾"	7½"
Shakes		
18"	—	7½"
24"	—	10"

Shingle exposures are for Number 1 (Blue Label) shingles only.

Wood Shingles & Shakes

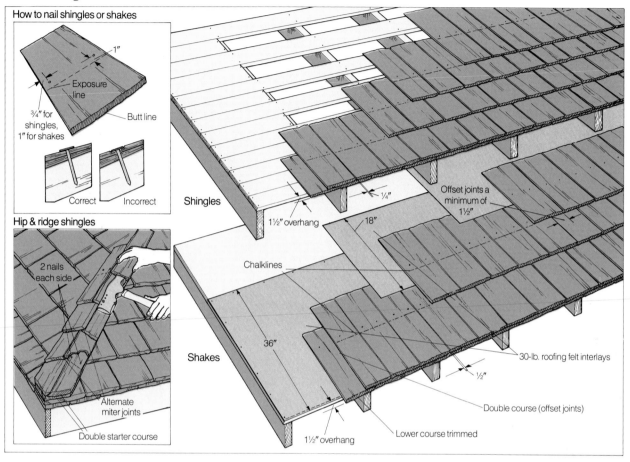

How to nail shingles or shakes

1"

Exposure line

Butt line

¾" for shingles, 1" for shakes

Correct   Incorrect

Hip & ridge shingles

2 nails each side

Alternate miter joints

Double starter course

Shingles

1½" overhang

Chalklines

Shakes

36"

Offset joints a minimum of 1½"

¼"

18"

30-lb. roofing felt interlays

½"

Double course (offset joints)

Lower course trimmed

1½" overhang

Nailing. For wood shingles and shakes, use rustproof nails, two per shingle or shake. For wood shingles, use 14½-gauge nails with ⁷⁄₃₂-inch-wide heads, 1¼ inches in length. For wood shakes, the preferred choice is 13-gauge nails with ⁷⁄₃₂-inch-wide heads, 2 inches long. (Check that nails won't poke through the sheathing and show from below.)

When fastening shingles, place the nails ¾ inch in from each side; nails for shakes are positioned 1 inch in from the sides. The nails should be 1 inch above the butt line for the next course.

Trimming shingles and shakes. To make straight cuts along the grain of shingles or thin shakes, simply slice through them with a roofer's hatchet. Heavier wood shakes must be sawn.

When it's necessary to cut a shingle or shake across the grain, lay it in place and use a utility knife to score the cut. If the wood is thin, break it against a hard edge. Otherwise, you'll have to saw it.

Starter course and first course. Though roofing felt is seldom required under wood shingles, it is recommended with shakes, because their irregular shape allows water to work through the cracks. If you're roofing with wood shakes, first nail a 36-inch-wide strip of 30-pound felt along the eave (allow a ⅜-inch overhang).

Combine the starter and first courses by laying the shingles or shakes one on top of the other, as shown above. Overhang this double course 1½ inches at the eaves and rakes. Offset the joints between layers a minimum of 1½ inches. Allow ¼ inch between shingles and ½ inch between shakes to permit the wood to expand and contract.

Successive courses. When you lay the next courses, align shingles or shakes both vertically and horizontally for proper exposure and coverage.

You don't need to snap chalklines for vertical alignment. Simply lay the random-width wood materials according to this principle: offset joints at least 1½ inches so that no joints in any three successive courses are in alignment.

To align wood shingles horizontally, snap a chalkline at the proper exposure over the doubled starter/first course or use your roofer's hatchet as an exposure guide. Then lay the lower edge of the next course on the chalkline and nail. Repeat, working your way up the roof, until you reach the ridge.

For wood shakes, you'll have to install roofing felt over each course as you work. From the bottom edge of the starter/first course, measure a distance twice the planned exposure. Place the bottom edge of an 18-inch-wide strip of 30-pound felt at that line and nail every 12 inches along the top edge of the felt. Overlap vertical joints 4 inches.

Then snap a chalkline on the starter/ first course for the proper exposure (or use your roofer's hatchet for a guide). Nail the second course, place the next felt, and continue until you reach the ridge. Use short, 15-inch shakes as the last course. Buy them ready-made or cut them from standard shakes.

At the ridge, let the last courses of shingles or shakes hang over; snap a chalkline above the center of the ridgeboard and trim all the ends at once. Cover the ridge with a strip of 30-pound felt at least 8 inches wide.

Applying hip and ridge shingles. Using factory-made ridge and hip shingles (mitering and making your own specialty shingles is a time-consuming task), double the starter courses at the bottom of each hip and at the end of the ridge, as shown on page 89 (bottom).

Exposure should equal the weather exposure of the wood shingles or shakes on the roof planes. Start the ridge shingles at the end of the ridge opposite prevailing winds. Use nails long enough (usually 2 to 2½ inches) to extend into the ridgeboard.

Roofing with Solid-Board Siding

Though it may not keep out wind-driven rain when used on a roof, bevel or Dolly Varden board siding is a roofing material that looks good both on top and underneath. You simply cut and nail horizontal boards directly onto the rafters. Or, for a more watertight application, you can mount siding boards onto roof sheathing that has been covered with underlayment (see page 85). A typical application is shown above.

Be sure the roof has a pitch of at least 4 in 12 (see page 85); a lower pitch may allow water to penetrate.

Nailing. Always use rustproof nails when applying solid-board siding and make sure they're long enough to pene-

Board Siding Roofing

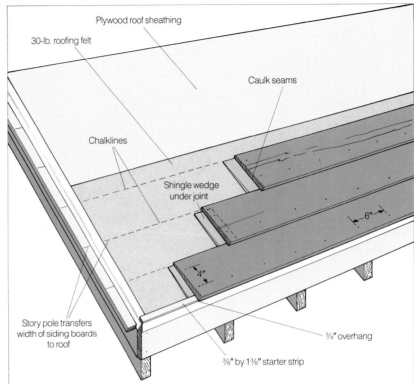

Plywood roof sheathing
30-lb. roofing felt
Caulk seams
Chalklines
Shingle wedge under joint
6"
4"
Story pole transfers width of siding boards to roof
¾" overhang
⅜" by 1⅜" starter strip

trate the rafters by at least 1 inch. Spiral or ring-shank nails offer better holding power than nails with smooth shanks. If the boards tend to split when nailed, predrill nail holes or slightly blunt nail tips before nailing.

Applying the first board. First, nail a starter strip along the roof's edge. This will push the first board out to match the angle of the other boards. Position the first board so it overhangs the starter strip ¾ inch. Then nail it in place, 1 inch from the lower edge.

Nailing successive boards. To lay out the rest of the boards, make a "story pole" from a 1 by 3 that's as long as the roof is deep. Mark the pole at intervals that equal the width of the siding boards; then transfer the marks to the edges of the roof. Apply the siding boards from bottom to top. Overlap each board 1 inch (or as per rabbeted edge) and nail every 6 inches, placing nails 1 inch from the lower edge.

Where boards will be end-joined,

brush water repellent, stain, or primer on the ends before installation and be sure to make the joint square and snug. Slip a shingle wedge under the joint and nail each board end to it, using two nails spaced 4 inches apart; caulk the seams. Though sidings don't have special pieces for hips and ridges, you can use cedar hip and ridge shingles. Flash as you would a shingle roof (see page 86).

Installing Plywood Siding

Some types of plywood are suitable for patio roofing (an underlayment of 30-pound roofing felt will help repel water). To minimize leaks, be sure the roof has a pitch of at least 4 in 12 (see page 85).

Though roofing felt and plywood can be applied directly over rafters, eliminating the need for bracing and sheathing, this type of installation won't be very attractive from below unless the structure has a ceiling to hide your view of the felt. The easiest way to build a ceiling is to nail ⅜-inch plywood sheets to the undersides of rafters.

Plywood Roofing

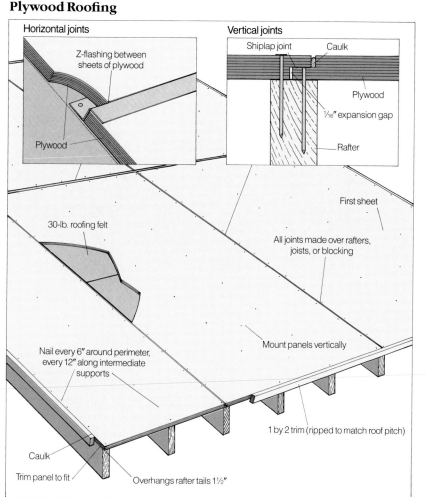

Horizontal joints

Z-flashing between sheets of plywood

Plywood

Vertical joints

Shiplap joint   Caulk

Plywood

$\frac{1}{16}$" expansion gap

Rafter

First sheet

All joints made over rafters, joists, or blocking

30-lb. roofing felt

Mount panels vertically

Nail every 6" around perimeter, every 12" along intermediate supports

1 by 2 trim (ripped to match roof pitch)

Caulk

Trim panel to fit

Overhangs rafter tails 1½"

Installing Corrugated Plastic & Aluminum Panels

Corrugated panels made from plastic or aluminum can provide reasonably watertight roofing on slopes as low as 2 in 12 (see page 85). The panels, 26 inches wide, are installed with a 2-inch overlap; they're designed to connect to rafters on 24-inch centers. The panels should be supported along the seams for both strength and appearance.

In addition, cross bracing is required every 5 feet between rafters to prevent sagging.

Cutting and nailing. You can cut plastic or aluminum panels with a fine-toothed handsaw or a power saw equipped with a plywood-cutting or abrasive blade. Caution: Be sure to wear eye protection when cutting.

Predrill nail holes, backing the panel with a scrap block as you drill. Special aluminum twist nails with neoprene washers under the head are made for plastic and aluminum panels. Be sure to nail through the crowns of the corrugations as shown below, not through the valleys. Nail every 12 inches.

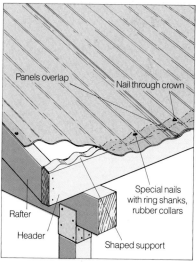

Panels overlap

Nail through crown

Special nails with ring shanks, rubber collars

Rafter

Header

Shaped support

Plywood siding applied directly to rafters without sheathing should be at least ½ inch thick if rafters are on 16-inch centers and at least ⅝ inch thick for rafters on 24-inch centers. Be sure to choose a siding pattern that will allow water to run off without interruption and that has vertical shiplap edges.

Plan to mount sheets vertically and to install sheet metal Z-flashing along any horizontal joints. Allow a $\frac{1}{16}$-inch expansion gap between sheets and caulk all seams. Before installing the plywood, brush the edges with water repellent, primer, or stain.

Nailing. Nail the sheets with rustproof common or box nails long enough to penetrate the rafters 1½ inches. Nail every 6 inches around the perimeter of

each sheet (at the rafters) and every 12 inches along intermediate supports.

Applying the first sheet. Position the first sheet at an outside corner, letting its lower edge overhang rafter tails 1½ inches along the eaves. Center the inside edge over a rafter, checking to be sure you've oriented the shiplap edge properly. Then mark and trim (using a circular saw or handsaw) the outer edge so it will overhang the rake about 1½ inches. Nail the sheet in place.

Installing successive sheets. Butt the next sheet against the first, interlocking the shiplap edges (if the panels have them) and leaving a $\frac{1}{16}$-inch expansion gap. Nail the sheet and caulk the seams. Apply remaining sheets in the same way.

To make joints watertight where they overlap, sandwich a bead of caulking compound between the lapped edges before you nail. Generally, the best caulks for this purpose are those that remain flexible (see page 94).

Customizing your patio roof or gazebo with built-in or freestanding benches, trellises for flowering vines, or outdoor lighting can make it more comfortable—and practical—for use during the day and into the evening. Adding any of these features is well within the capability of the do-it-yourselfer. The instructions below will help you get started.

Seating

Though commercial benches and other garden seating are readily available, designing and building your own allows you to blend in the seating with your overhead's design and, in many cases, to take advantage of posts or other support members for partial support. A few bench ideas are illustrated below.

Design considerations. When designing a bench, keep in mind that, for maximum comfort, the seat should be 15 to 18 inches high, the approximate height or slightly lower than most chairs. If you plan to use a thick mat or cushion, lower the seat to allow for it.

There is no set guide for depth. A bench only 12 inches deep, though common, is more a place to perch than a place to relax. A depth of 15 to 18 inches is comfortable, but you can make the seat even deeper for lounging—24 inches is the width of most standard lounge pads.

Legs or supporting members should be sturdy enough for solid support and still be in scale with the rest of the bench. If the legs are made from 4 by 4s or a material of similar strength, space them 3 to 5 feet apart. If you're using a lighter-weight material or if the lumber for the top of the seat needs additional support to prevent it from sagging, place the legs closer together.

Be sure to allow for a kickspace underneath the seat. Not being able to tuck your feet under can be very uncomfortable.

For strength, use 2-by lumber for bench seats. Though a single wide plank, such as a 2 by 12, looks stronger than two 2 by 6s or three 2 by 4s, the wide plank has a greater tendency to warp or split. If your plans call for planks 8 inches or more in width, be sure to choose well-seasoned ones and face them crown sides down. Always use surfaced lumber for seating.

Building tips. Prebore holes for screws and bolts, and countersink them so the heads don't extend above the surface. If you're using finishing nails, set the nail heads below the surface, using a nailset.

Sand or plane any exposed surfaces smooth and round off edges. Treat with stain or paint (see page 95) to minimize the effects of weathering.

Trellises

Trellises offer support to young shrubs or vines. And when a plant is splayed out in graceful curves and masses against a background grid, it often looks more attractive and displays its flowers or fruits better than when it's allowed to grow freely in all directions. A framework that holds a plant away from the wall also keeps it healthier, since good air circulation minimizes mildew and rot.

Rampant growers like honeysuckle can benefit from the discipline of a sturdy trellis. The framework offers the vine some alternative to filling every crack and crevice in a fence or wall, and it encourages a gardener to keep the vine trimmed back. (Almost all plants need more pruning and pinching when grown on a trellis than when grown elsewhere.)

Finally, the trellis itself adds year-round interest, especially if it provides some color contrast with its environment.

The examples on pages 54–55 show a few trellises you can build. Construct them with care, using good materials

Ideas for Benches

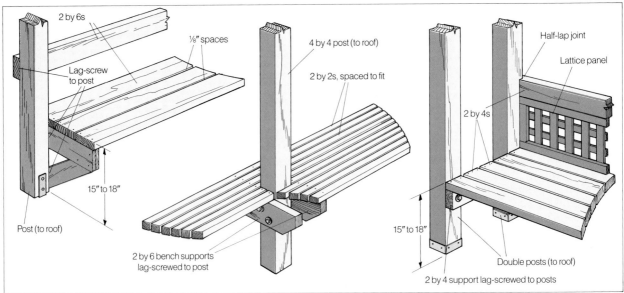

2 by 6s
⅛" spaces
Lag-screw to post
15" to 18"
Post (to roof)

4 by 4 post (to roof)
2 by 2s, spaced to fit
2 by 6 bench supports lag-screwed to post

Half-lap joint
Lattice panel
2 by 4s
15" to 18"
Double posts (to roof)
2 by 4 support lag-screwed to posts

VINES FOR TRELLISES

Vines aren't necessary components of every garden, but when climbing up a trellis or clinging to a lath overhead, they often add just the right finishing touch. Here is a list of some vines that may grow successfully in your garden. The figures in parentheses following the names are the minimum temperatures the plants can withstand.

Anemone clematis *(C. montana)* (-10°). This deciduous, fast-growing vine puts on a lavish white to pink floral display in early spring just before its leaves emerge. A vigorous climber, its light green leaves provide moderate to dense shade. The plant requires regular watering and light pruning.

Blood-red trumpet vine *(Distictis buccinatoria,* sometimes sold as *Phaedranthus buccinatorius)* (24°). A rapidly growing evergreen vine, this plant blooms brilliantly when the weather is warm; its trumpet-shaped flowers are orange red fading to bluish red. It provides moderate shade.

Bougainvillea (30°). Though the peak flowering period comes in summer, blooms—in dazzling, neon-bright colors of purple, magenta, crimson, brick red, orange, yellow, pink, or white—may appear from spring through autumn (even into the winter) in the mildest climates. A fast, vigorous grower with medium green leaves, this evergreen vine supplies moderate to dense shade.

Clematis jackmanii (-20°). Though it provides only very light shade, this clematis freely produces large purple flowers in summer. Dormant stems must be cut back as new growth starts in March.

Common white jasmine, poet's jasmine *(Jasminum officinale)* (5°). This rapidly growing evergreen vine loses some of its foliage in colder regions. Fragrant white flowers bloom throughout the spring. After blooming, the vine must be thinned and pruned to maintain its attractiveness.

Evergreen clematis *(Clematis armandii)* (0°). A slow starter, evergreen clematis grows rapidly later on and provides light to moderate shade. Its glossy, dark green foliage droops downward to create a strongly textured pattern; flowers, which appear in spring, are fragrant, white, and star shaped. After blooming, this vine needs pruning to keep it in check.

Giant Burmese honeysuckle *(Lonicera hildebrandiana)* (20°). This plant's dark green leaves provide moderate shade. Fragrant summer flowers up to 7 inches long are white when they open, turning yellow to soft orange as they age. A fast-growing evergreen, honeysuckle requires a lot of water.

Grapes (American, -25°; European, 10°). The luxuriant foliage of this deciduous, rapidly growing vine produces dense, cool shade. Fruiting varieties provide edible grapes but also may attract insects.

Roses (0°). Vining roses provide light to moderate amounts of shade and usually grow rapidly. Many varieties are available; choose disease-resistant types with good quality foliage.

Sweet autumn clematis *(Clematis dioscoreifolia robusta,* formerly *C. paniculata)* (-10°). From late summer into autumn, this deciduous vine offers frothy masses of small, fragrant, creamy white flowers against glossy, dark green leaves. It grows quickly and provides moderate to heavy shade.

Wisteria (-30°). Fragrant, pendulous clusters of white, pink, lavender, or purple flowers characterize wisteria in spring. The light green foliage, which appears later, provides moderate to heavy amounts of shade.

and strong galvanized nails, bolts, and screws. Growing plants can exert a lot of force, and the weight of a mature plant can be much greater than expected. For some suggestions of vines you can use, see the listing above.

Outdoor Lighting

To extend the hours you can use an outdoor area, to shed light on an outdoor food preparation area, or to illuminate plants or paths, outdoor lighting is a welcome addition to any landscaping plan.

One method of providing outdoor lighting is to extend your home's 120-volt system into the garden to power a variety of permanently placed fixtures (be sure to check with your building department for code requirements). Or you can step the system down to 12 volts and use lightweight, movable fixtures.

If you're thinking of adding outdoor lights to an existing or new circuit, have an electrician help you plan and install the system.

The advantages of a 12-volt system over a 120-volt one are easy installation and less danger from harmful shock. No electrical permit is required to install a 12-volt system that extends from a low-voltage plug-in transformer.

Installing a 12-volt system is simple: you mount a transformer near the power source and run cable from the transformer to the desired locations for your lights. The low-voltage fixtures attach directly to the wiring. Some simply clip onto the wire; others must be wired into the system. No grounding connections are required.

Most transformers for outdoor lights are encased in watertight boxes, but to be safe, plan to install yours in a sheltered location at least a foot off the ground. The cable can lie on top of the ground or be fastened to wood support members.

Sooner or later, wood's natural enemies — insects, weather, and decay-causing organisms — will attack any wooden structure. However, treating wood with a preservative and/or finish can add years to a structure's useful life and keep it looking good. Even heart-grade redwood, cedar, and cypress, disease-resistant as they are, benefit from treatment.

Wood preservatives serve mainly as protection against decay. Many have no effect on appearance. Those that do usually leave a discoloration that must be covered with paint or stain. Some wood is pressure-treated with preservatives before it even reaches the lumberyard; in other cases, a preservative is applied just before construction or as a primer under a finish.

Caulking compounds fill exterior cracks or seams that might otherwise let in damaging moisture and invasive insects.

Finishes, usually paints or stains, protect against weathering. Some do double duty, guarding against decay. These do affect appearance—changing color, hiding wood grain, and sometimes even masking wood texture.

The degree of protection and the type of finish you need for your overhead depend on several factors, among them climate, moisture, and the grade and species of the wood. Severe weather, especially cold, can result in checking, splitting, warping, or other related problems. Constant exposure to moisture allows fungi and bacteria to flourish. And the different species and grades of wood vary in their resistance to decay.

Wood Preservatives

Pressure treatment, the most effective method of preservative application, forces chemical preservatives deep into wood fibers. Through pressure treatment, lumber from species such as southern pine or Douglas fir can be made as durable as the hardier types — redwood, cedar, and cypress.

When you're shopping for pressure-treated lumber, look for a quality mark from the American Wood Preservers Bureau (AWPB); this mark, shown on page 71, assures you that the treatment has met established standards and offers information about the wood's proper use. Depending on the amount of chemical injected, the wood may be labeled "ground-contact" use or "above-ground" use.

Preservatives can also be applied with a brush or by immersion (in a large bucket or drum), but the long-term results are less satisfactory.

If you plan to apply a preservative yourself, talk with your building-supply dealer about the types that are both effective and safe to use. (Two once-popular preservatives, pentachlorophenol and creosote, are no longer available to the consumer because of questions about possible health hazards resulting from their use.)

Copper naphthenate, a brush-on preservative, is quite effective. Because it's nontoxic to plants and animals, it's especially useful for treating garden structures. The dark green tinge it leaves on treated wood can be covered with two coats of paint.

Caulking Compounds

Caulking compounds vary in both price and composition. As a rule, you get what you pay for.

For most caulking jobs, a caulking gun with an 11-ounce cartridge (illustrated above, at right) is the simplest to use. Before applying caulk, make sure the surface is clean, dry, and free of oil and old caulking material. Check the manufacturer's instructions for any special requirements, and, if you plan to paint or stain over it, be sure to choose a "paintable" caulk.

Appropriate caulking compounds are described below. Oil-base caulks are not recommended for outdoor use.

Elastomeric caulks. These synthetic "supercaulks" are the top of the line. They effectively seal almost any type of crack or joint, they adhere to most materials, and they'll outlast ordinary caulks by many years. The generic types that fall into this category include polysulfides, polyurethanes, and silicones.

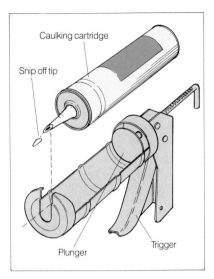

To use a caulking gun, snip off tip; puncture inner seal with a long nail.

These products do have a few drawbacks, in addition to cost. Silicone rubber is awkward to smooth out once applied and may not readily accept paint. Polysulfide can't be used on porous surfaces unless a special primer is applied first.

Latex and butyl-rubber caulks. These all-purpose caulks offer average performance at an average price. Included in this category are latex, acrylic latex, and butyl-rubber.

Latex and acrylic latex caulks vary in price and performance. The acrylic latex caulks outperform nonacrylic latexes. Both are easy to apply, and both clean up with water.

Butyl-rubber caulk, generally more flexible and durable than acrylic latex, can be used on any type of surface or material. It has a tendency to shrink slightly while curing.

Wood Finishes

Finishes differ from preservatives in that they're deliberate choices for altering the natural appearance of wood. Also, all preservatives penetrate wood, whereas some finishes — notably paint — form a film around it. Your choices in finishes include clear water repellents, stains, and paints.

Clear water repellents. Also known as water seals, clear water repellents are a suitable initial treatment for any raw wood. They penetrate into the wood's fibers and provide a clear barrier to moisture. They can also provide an extra layer of protection over stains.

Stains. Stains are available in two color intensities: semitransparent types contain enough pigment to tint the wood surface but not enough to hide the natural grain; solid-color stains contain more pigment—many appear to be almost as opaque as paint (they're excellent for masking lower grades of lumber). But because stains penetrate rather than forming a film, as paint does, they don't cover the texture of the wood.

Stains come in a variety of colors ranging from pale gray through the darkest wood colors. Paint and building supply stores keep sample chips indicating colors. However, these can give only a general idea. How your choice performs depends on your wood and the weather in your area.

In general, stain looks best on rough or saw-textured lumber. On any surface, rough or smooth, stains may require periodic refinishing because of wear or weathering.

A recommended staining method is to pretreat the lumber with clear water repellent and then apply stain after the structure has been up about a month. Or, if you're using an opaque stain, you can prestain the lumber and touch it up with a second coat when the structure has been completed.

Heavy-bodied stains may be either brushed or sprayed on. Light-bodied types are sprayed on and then brushed smooth, or applied in two coats using a brush only.

Paints. Paints can create solid color effects from muted to vibrant and permit the use of lower grades of lumber since their opaque quality masks defects.

Today, most painters recommend a two-step procedure for outdoor structures: first, an alkyd- or oil-base prime coat followed by one or two topcoats of water-base (latex) enamel. The prime coat is imperative for redwood or western red cedar (water-base primers or paints may dissolve extractives in these woods, discoloring the paint). Also, be sure the primer doesn't contain zinc oxide.

For the longest-lasting finish, pretreat the lumber with water repellent and apply the primer before erecting the roof. Wait several days between soaking the wood with water repellent and applying the primer. Primer should cover all lumber surfaces, including the inner faces of built-up posts, beams, or rafters. Apply topcoats after the structure has been completed.

Pay special attention to the chemical compatibility of the water repellent, primer, and top coat. Be sure that the manufacturer's recommendations apply specifically to the kinds of treatment and finish you're using. Buying materials made by the same manufacturer gives you a head start on compatibility; even so, be sure to check all labels to assure workable combinations.

Because heat may create drying problems and dust, leading to marred or roughened surfaces, try to paint on a cool, windless day. In hot, dry weather, paint only after the sun is low so drying can be slow.

Before painting, always sweep or dust surfaces, and be sure they're dry. If the wood is painted while it's moist, the paint may fail to bond, leading to blistering or other failure. Apply paint with either a brush or roller.

Paint brings color, vibrancy, and durability to poolside structure. Angled rafter cuts in pyramid-shaped roof give it a jewel-like quality. Landscape architect: Ed Haag.

■ INDEX

PROJECT PLANS

In the preceding chapters you've seen architectural details and construction techniques for a wide variety of gazebos and patio roofs. For an even broader selection of outdoor structures, this appendix offers an additional collection of project plans that you can purchase. Included are gazebos, deck/gazebo combinations, patio covers, and screened porch additions. With these plans in hand, you can tackle a building project yourself or hire a professional carpenter or builder to do the work. Pages 98 and 99 provide information on how to order plans, including suggestions on the number of copies you will need, pricing, and an order form. Simply choose the plan that's right for you from the descriptions beginning on page 100, and then place your order.

BEFORE YOU ORDER

Plan packages for the projects on the following pages include all of the information you'll need to successfully build the projects. When you order a plan set, you will receive complete, large-scale drawings, details, and specifications. The plans call out part sizes, and most present detailed step-by-step instructions for assembly. Several offer plans for alternate sizes, enabling you to adapt the project to suit your outdoor living space. Before filling out the order form on the following page, note the information that follows.

HOW MANY PLAN SETS WILL YOU NEED?

Each plan package contains two complete sets of plans. Though a single set should suffice for a simple project, such as the smaller gazebos and patio covers, the spare set may come in handy if you like to make modifications or scribble notes on your plans. For more complex designs, you may need several sets, particularly if you intend to obtain bids from two or three builders or carpenters.

If your building department requires a permit for a structure such as the Screened Porch Addition, figure you will need one set each for yourself, the building department, and any builders or subcontractors involved in the project.

SERVICE AND PLAN DELIVERY

Company service representatives are available to answer questions and assist you in placing your order. Every possible effort is made to process and ship orders within 48 hours.

RETURNS AND EXCHANGES

Each set of project plans is specially printed and shipped to you based on your specific order; consequently, requests for refunds cannot be honored. However, if the prints you order cannot be used, you may exchange them for another plan. For an exchange, you must return all sets of plans within 30 days. A nonrefundable service charge will be assessed for all exchanges; for more information, call our toll-free number (1-800-721-7027).

COMPLIANCE WITH LOCAL CODES AND REGULATIONS

Because of climatic, geographic, and political variations, building codes and regulations vary to some extent from one area to another. These plans are authorized for your use expressly conditioned on your obligation and agreement to comply strictly with all local building codes, ordinances, regulations, and requirements, including permits and inspections at the time of construction.

LICENSE AGREEMENT, COPY RESTRICTIONS, AND COPYRIGHT

When you purchase your plans, you are granted the right to use the documents to construct a single unit only.

All the plans in this publication are protected under the Federal Copyright Act, Title XVII of the United States Code and Chapter 37 of the Code of Federal Regulations. Each designer retains title and ownership of the original documents. The plans licensed to you cannot be used by or resold to any other person, copied, or reproduced by any means. If you require additional plans, you must order additional packets (again, each packet contains two complete sets of plans).

Complete the order form on the following page in three easy steps. Then mail in your order, or, for faster service, call our toll-free number (1-800-721-7027).

ORDERING PLANS

1. PLANS AND ACCESSORIES

Price Code	Description	Price
A	Small projects and accessories	$12.95
B	Patio covers	$15.95
C	Simple gazebos and porch additions	$19.95
D	Classic gazebos and gazebo/deck combinations	$24.95

Prices subject to change

Each plan package contains two sets of plans

2. SHIPPING AND HANDLING

Determine shipping and handling charges from the chart below.

Shipping and Handling Charges

Type of Service*	Plan Package	2 Plan Packages	3 Plan Packages
U.S. Regular	$ 4.95	$ 7.95	$ 9.95
U.S. Express	$12.50	$15.50	$18.50
Canada Regular	$ 7.45	$ 9.95	$12.45
Canada Express	$18.00	$20.50	$23.00

* U.S. Regular (4–6 working days)
U.S. Express (2–3 working days)
Canada Regular (2–3 weeks)
Canada Express (7–10 working days)

3. CUSTOMER INFORMATION

Choose the method of payment you prefer. Include a check, money order, or credit card information, complete the name and address portion, and mail the order form to:

Sunset/HomeStyles Plan Service
P.O. Box 75488
St. Paul, MN 55175-0488

**For faster service, call
1-800-721-7027**

PLAN CHECKLIST

Plan number(s) _____ **Price code(s)** _____

Number of packages _____ $ _____
(see chart at left)

Subtotal $ _____
Sales tax (Minnesota residents only, add 6.5%) $ _____
Shipping and handling $ _____
GRAND TOTAL $ _____

☐ Check/money order enclosed (in U.S. funds)
☐ VISA ☐ MasterCard ☐ AmEx ☐ Discover

Credit card # _____

Exp. Date _____

Signature _____

Name _____

Address_____

City _____ State/Province _____

Country _____

Zip/Postal code_____

Daytime phone (___)_____

Please check if you are a contractor ☐

Mail form to: Sunset/HomeStyles Plan Service
P.O. Box 75488
St. Paul, MN 55175-0488

Or fax to: 651-602-5002

**FOR FASTER SERVICE,
CALL 1-800-721-7027
INTERNATIONAL CALL
651-602-5003**

Source code: SSPPO5

OCTAGON GAZEBO

HDA-13001
PRICE CODE D
- 11'6" × 11'6"
- Height, floor to peak: 14'7"
- Plenty of space for outdoor entertaining

VICTORIAN GAZEBO

HPM-1603
PRICE CODE D
- Large, triangle-shaped gazebo
- Each side is 16' long
- Elegantly detailed

GARDEN GAZEBO

AB-1692
PRICE CODE D
- 12' × 12'
- Easy to build
- Handsome lattice panels

CLASSIC GAZEBO

HPM-1601
PRICE CODE D
- 16' across the floor
- Detailed materials list
- Construction guidelines

LARGE GAZEBO AND DECK

L-1-PAV
PRICE CODE D

- 34' × 22'
- Elegant entertainment structure
- Ideal for a large, sloping lot

COUNTRY GAZEBO

HPM-1600
PRICE CODE D

- 10' × 13'
- Unique and private
- Detailed instructions

SALTBOX GAZEBO

HPM-1602
PRICE CODE D

- 10'8" × 14'
- Spacious interior
- Easy-to-use plans

CONTEMPORARY GAZEBO

HPM-1604
PRICE CODE D

- 16' across
- Vaulted roof
- Unobtrusive structure
  for any backyard

TRADITIONAL SIX-SIDED GAZEBO

HDA-13028
PRICE CODE C

- 9'10" × 8'8"
- Height, floor to peak: 10'9"
- Ideal for small gatherings

PICTURESQUE GAZEBO

AB-1674
PRICE CODE C

- 9' × 12'
- Stylish curved roof
- Simple construction

COZY SIX-SIDED GAZEBO

HDA-13019
PRICE CODE C

- 8'3" × 9'6"
- Height, floor to peak: 12'10"
- Picturesque in a small corner of the garden

SIMPLE VICTORIAN GAZEBO

AB-1673
PRICE CODE C

- 9$\frac{1}{2}$' × 7$\frac{1}{2}$'
- Easy and inexpensive to build
- Perfect for a children's play area

GARDEN GAZEBO WITH CUPOLA

SOM-8010
PRICE CODE D

- Three sizes included: 10' × 10', 12' × 12', and 16' × 16'
- Open air, screen, and window designs
- Girder, pier, and rim beam details included

NOSTALGIC GAZEBO

SOM-8020
PRICE CODE D

- Plans for three different sizes: 9', 12', and 16'
- Elegant design for use throughout the seasons
- Step-by-step instructions

DECK WITH GAZEBO

HDA-13002
PRICE CODE D

- 24' × 15'6"
- Height, floor to peak: 12'2"
- Enjoy your deck year-round with a shaded gazebo for outdoor eating and special events

DECK RAILINGS—5 STYLES

HDA-13023
PRICE CODE A

- Includes plans for five styles: contemporary (double and single bevel), colonial, and traditional 2' × 2' and 2' × 4'
- Easily adaptable to any outdoor structure

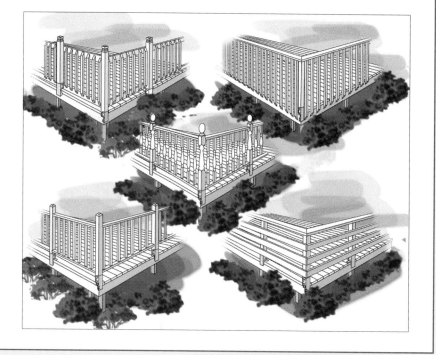

TIERED DECK WITH GAZEBO

HDA-13031
PRICE CODE D

- Deck: 28'6" × 15'6"
- Gazebo: 8' across with roof and side railings
- Sprawling outdoor entertaining area with three decks, a walkway, and a cozy gazebo

TRELLIS DECK

AB-1378
PRICE CODE B

- Overhead structure for welcome shade
- Four different sizes included: 16' × 20', 16' × 16', 14' × 20', and 14' × 16'
- Complete materials list

EASY PATIO COVER

HDA-13016
PRICE CODE B

- 16' × 12'
- Features a sun screen covering
- Adds beauty and value to your home

PATIO ROOF AND SUN SHADE COVERS

HDA-13026
PRICE CODE B

- Patio roof size: 16' × 9'
- Sun shade size: 20' × 10'
- Two easy to build plans, whether you want protection from the rain or the sun

FREESTANDING PATIO COVERS

HDA-13015
PRICE CODE B

- Plans for two sizes: 12' × 12' and 16' × 12'
- Designed to cover an existing deck or patio
- Can also be used as a pavilion without a deck floor

ENTRANCE ARBORS

SOM-3001
PRICE CODE B

- Four different designs: Sunburst Arbor, Arched Arbor, Classic Arbor, and Sunrise Arbor
- Detailed architectural plans

GARDEN ENTRYWAY

HDA-13018
PRICE CODE C

- 8' × 8'
- Height, floor to peak: 10'10"
- An elegant place to rest while enjoying the garden

PORCH ADDITION

AB-347
PRICE CODE C

- A 12' × 12' room
- The addition conforms to the siding on your home
- Detailed step-by-step instructions

SCREENED PORCH

HDA-15018
PRICE CODE C

- Porch size: 12'3" deep and 16'6" wide
- Enjoy the warm weather in comfort
- Built-in plant shelves

SCREENED PORCH ADDITION

HDA-15003
PRICE CODE C

- Porch size: 16' × 12'
- Easy-to-follow professional blueprints
- Dimensional drawings and details